The Complete Guide

Perthshire Paperweights

Magnum mushroom from the 1997 collection

The Complete Guide to
Perthshire
Paperweights

by Colin & Debby Mahoney
and Gary & Marge McClanahan

Photo Credits

Stuart Drysdale Memorial Weight: courtesy of **Bergstrom-Mahler Museum**
                                     Neenah, Wisconsin

Perthshire factory: **Colin Mahoney**
                             Peter McDougall
                             Perthshire Paperweights Limited

Paperweight photos: **Gary McClanahan**

Layout: **Colin Mahoney**

Reprint 2015
Several spelling and typographical errors were corrected.
International Standard Book Number: 978-1516944439
Published by Colin Mahoney

Originally published in Santa Cruz, CA in 1997
Library of Congress Catalog Card Number: 97-66591

Preface

Perthshire Paperweights Limited celebrated its 25th Anniversary in 1993. To commemorate this occasion, the Southern California and San Diego Chapters of the Paperweight Collectors Association (PCA) jointly sponsored an anniversary exhibit, wherein all of the production weights ever made by Perthshire were put on display for the first time. The reason for such a display was quite simple. A large number of collectors can honestly say that Perthshire paperweights were among the very first fine paperweights they collected. These collectors feel that Perthshire paperweights got them started as "serious" collectors. The authors were no exception. They started their collections with Perthshire paperweights and came to appreciate their artistry as well as variety. They also managed to assemble the only known complete collection of Perthshire paperweights. The authors wrote an exhibit guide (without pictures), which was printed for the 1993 event.

At the completion of the one-day anniversary exhibit in 1993 and during the time since then, many collectors have requested that the exhibit catalog be expanded into a full-color, comprehensive guide to Perthshire paperweights. This book is the response to those many requests.

The 1997 convention of the Paperweight Collectors Association was held in San Diego, California, and the entire Perthshire collection was once again exhibited. The display included more than 500 paperweights and related items. That complete exhibit is documented in this book.

The authors hope that this guide will prove to be a valuable reference for paperweight collectors everywhere and that its use will enhance the enjoyment of paperweight collecting by all who read it.

Special weight made for the 1993 exhibit

Acknowledgments

The authors would like to thank all those who contributed information and documentation or loaned paperweights so that the photographic record could be complete.

We would specially like to thank **Neil Drysdale**, Managing Director of Perthshire Paperweights Limited, and **Peter McDougall**, Factory Manager, for supplying technical advice, reference and research materials, factory photos, and specific paperweights that enabled us to compile much of the detailed information about Perthshire.

Thanks also to **Roger Jacobsen** and to **Harvey and Doris Robinson** for the copies of much of the early Perthshire factory literature that enabled us to know what we were looking for when we were assembling a complete collection to commemorate the 25th Anniversary of Perthshire Paperweights Limited in 1993.

The authors also thank the following collectors who loaned weights for photographs in this book.

Dr. M. Arthur Grant: Alternate colors of several weights

Roger Jacobsen: Blue 1970B Flash Overlay

Jane A. Jonscher: Council Tree letter opener

Brian and Ruth Mahoney: "Personal" weight

Barry Schultheiss: Closepacked millefiori newel post

D.C. Smith: One-of-a-kind mushroom weight with millefiori ring

John and Patricia Vandersall: PP14 weight with the letter "A"

Table of Contents

Annual Collection

Christmas Weights

Limited Edition and
General Range

Special Editions

Paperweight-related Items

One-of-a-kind Weights

Dedication

This book is dedicated to the memory of Stuart Drysdale, without whose vision, efforts, and dedication, the very existence of Perthshire Paperweights Limited would not be. All who were privileged to have known him, whether as manager and boss, as he was to the artists and employees of Perthshire Paperweights, or as business man and salesman, as he was to the many dealers and collectors around the world, he was first of all a friend.

In 1967, when he was shown an issue of a magazine which featured an article about the fine French paperweights in the Bergstrom Art Center, his goal became to create modern paperweights that would equal the very finest of these antiques. While the artists and craftsmen were quick to say that they could make paperweights as good as those fine antiques, it was just as quickly proven that there was indeed much to learn and a long way to go from that early start.

It was Stuart Drysdale who met the many challenges of business, for without the business side, Perthshire could not have succeeded. And it was he who set the standards that only the highest quality would be the minimum acceptable level of achievement. Stuart's guidance was paramount in putting Perthshire Paperweights at the top of the list of modern paperweight factories.

This book is the proof that Stuart Drysdale's 1967 goal of having Perthshire's paperweights be the equal of the very best of the antique weights has indeed been accomplished.

Stuart Drysdale Memorial Weight on display at the Bergstrom-Mahler Museum

Introduction

Of all the media available to the creative artist, glass is without a doubt one of the most interesting. Its ability to be formed into endless shapes and the way it reacts with light to transmit and alter colors make it a wondrous material for the most inventive and talented artist. Within all of the forms of art glass, the paperweight is often referred to as the "highest form of the glassworker's art." Perthshire paperweights are most certainly some of the finest examples of the paperweight makers' art.

Perthshire paperweights can be called the ideal collectible. This is true for a number of reasons. Foremost, they have a very high artistic and technical quality. Perthshire paperweights are made in a variety of styles and in a wide range of prices, suiting both the beginning and sophisticated collector. The wide range available allows the collector to choose between developing a complete collection or focusing on an area of particular interest, e.g., lampwork flowers, millefiori canes and patterns, latticinio cushions, color grounds, double overlays, picture canes, miniatures, one-of-a-kind weights, or Christmas weights.

Since its beginning, the factory has issued documentation that is helpful to the collector in identifying weights and edition sizes. Annual catalogues from recent years are quite readily available to collectors, but literature from the 1970s and early 1980s is relatively scarce. The information on weights from these early years of Perthshire Paperweights Ltd. was researched and compiled by the authors during the development of their Perthshire collections. This book is a result of their desire to share this information with other collectors and to provide a complete reference on Perthshire paperweights.

In addition to being an identification guide to Perthshire paperweights, this book contains a brief summary of Perthshire's history and describes the factory's techniques for making paperweights and the millefiori canes that are one of the most recognized features of Perthshire weights. A comprehensive glossary is also included.

Possibly the section of the book that the collector will ultimately find most useful is the Catalogue, which, for the first time, forms a complete and comprehensive listing of all of the production designs ever made, as well as examples of the many Special Editions that have been produced. These include such editions as the Council Tree weights issued for the Bergstrom-Mahler Museum, the Spanish Armada and French Revolution weights issued to commemorate historical events, and the special designs like the Double Overlay Encased Double Overlay weights, the State Bird series, and the Crystal-encased Double Overlay weights.

Representative examples of many one-of-a-kind weights are also included, as are pictures of some of the paperweight-related items Perthshire has produced, such as bowls, letter openers, and jewelry. Every piece pictured in the Catalogue was made at the Perthshire factory at sometime during its history.

This book will enable the collector to identify a Perthshire paperweight by following a few simple steps and then comparing the weight to the pictures. There will always be variations and exceptions for which even the most knowledgeable experts cannot provide a positive attribution, but, in most cases, the guidelines and photos in this book will lead the reader to the proper identification, even if the paperweight in question is a variation of a standard design—or an unrecorded one-of-a-kind weight.

The Identification Chapter includes a number of tables that are useful in the identification process. These tables cover information such as the production years for each design and the relationship between the Perthshire alphabet "signatures" and the production year represented—e.g., "A" is 1969.

Most Perthshire weights are signed and many are dated. The descriptive text accompanying the picture of each weight indicates the type of signature and the dates specific for that design. Pictures of the various types of signatures and dates are included in the Identification Chapter.

The Catalogue is divided into separate sections for various categories of weights. In addition to the factory categories of "Annual Collection," "Limited Edition," and "General Range," separate categories have been added for Special Editions, Christmas Weights, Paperweight-related items and One-of-a-kind Weights. Letter designations for Annual Collection weights made before 1983 follow the order used in previous publications. For weights made since 1983, when Perthshire instituted the nomenclature of "1983A," 1983B," etc., factory designations are used. For convenience,

the Limited Edition and General Range weights are combined into one category since they share a Perthshire numbering system, i. e., "PP1," "PP2," etc. The detailed written description accompanying each picture will help the collector to see how the design was developed, thereby enabling a positive identification of even the most complex millefiori weights.

In cases where a single PP number has been used for more than one specific design, such as the PP46, which was issued as heart (three different designs), club, spade, and diamond designs, each separate design is shown. A few PP numbers such as the PP5 do not refer to a specific design. These are so identified and pictures of some representative designs are shown. Some weights, such as the PP12 and PP13 designs can be identified only by comparing the dates to the ground or lace colors. Pictures in the Catalogue and a comparison chart in the Identification Chapter will lead to a positive identification of these weights.

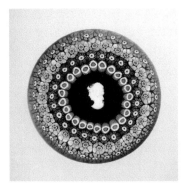

Perthshire sulphide

One-of-a-kind weights have been made throughout the history of the Perthshire factory. While several of these are pictured in this book, no effort was made to make this comprehensive, either as to types or designs. Certainly, hundreds

Long-cane closepack

of one-of-a-kind weights were made over the years. They cover the range from relatively simple pieces, such as the long-cane closepack and the sulphide weights which are pictured, to encased bouquets with fancy faceting, to the incredibly complex combinations of lampwork, millefiori, double or triple encasements, and elaborate cutting and faceting, all in the same magnum paperweight. A complete photographic record of all of the one-of-a-kind weights would fill a book by itself; however, since photographs of many of these pieces are not available, such a compilation would be impossible.

Silhouette and picture cane closepack

Special weights have been made upon request to honor and celebrate many events such as birthdays and weddings. Colin Mahoney's special "birthday closepack" of all silhouette and picture canes is

pictured as an example of this type of weight. (The factory says "never again!") "Personal" weights are also available by special order from the factory. These weights typically have a simple flower or bouquet with script lettering on a blue ground.

"Personal" weight

In many cases the available historical documentation is minimal at best, and at least one weight design that was shown in an early factory catalogue cannot be found. Nobody at the factory remembers that such a piece was actually produced. Other than that possible "missing link," the authors believe this book is a complete record of every Perthshire issue from the first "Annual Collection" weight, i.e., the 1969A Crown, through the PP185 issued in January 1997.

Information on weights issued after January 1997 can be obtained by writing to: Perthshire Paperweights Ltd., 14 Comrie Street, Crieff, Perthshire, Scotland PH7 4AZ. Visitors are welcome at the factory.

History

Perthshire Paperweights has enhanced Scottish glass making ever since its doors opened in 1968. However, Scottish paperweight making actually has its roots in Spain. In 1909 Spanish-born Salvador Ysart moved his family to France in search of work at the various glassworks. The First World War broke out in 1914 and, a year later, he decided to leave France in the interest of his family's safety. The Leith Flint Glass Company in Edinburgh, Scotland, recruited Salvador, and he and his eldest son, Paul, started work in Perth at John Moncrieff Ltd. in 1922. By 1937 all four of Salvador's sons worked there, producing the line of Monart Glassware.

From top to bottom: Salvador Ysart,
row 2: Vasart,
row 3: Strathearn,
row 4: early Perthshire

The Ysarts also produced some paperweights during this time period.

When World War II began in 1939, the Ysarts produced laboratory glassware. Salvador and his sons, Augustine and Vincent, left Moncrieff's in 1946 to set up on their own. They started Ysart Brothers Glass in Perth and made a line of glassware (including paperweights) called Vasart. The name came from the first letters of the first names: **V**incent, **A**ugustine and **S**alvador and from the last three letters in Y**sart**.

After the deaths of Salvador and Augustine, Vincent carried on the business alone. He renamed the company Vasart Glass Ltd. in 1956 and later collaborated with George Dunlop of Pirelli Glass in the making of gift-type glass, including paperweights. Vincent didn't like the administrative side of the business and persuaded Stuart Drysdale to become the manager in 1960. Under Stuart's guidance, Vasart Glass Ltd. prospered, and by 1964 a larger factory was needed.

Teacher's Whiskey became the majority owner of Vasart Glass Ltd. In 1965, the works moved from the old location in Perth to a new plant in Crieff. Teacher's named the new company Strathearn Glass, with Vincent Ysart as Works Manager and Stuart Drysdale as General Manager.

The Beginning

In 1967 Stuart Drysdale was sent a copy of a magazine containing photographs of antique paperweights. Stuart was intrigued by the many fine paperweights displayed in the magazine. He took it to the Strathearn factory and showed it to his glassworkers. They all said they "could do as well as that."

Also in 1967, Teacher's Whiskey decided to pursue a more abstract series of paperweight designs at Strathearn. This departure from the classic designs that were being made resulted in artistic differences between Stuart and Teacher's. So, in early 1968, Stuart and several of his glassworkers quietly went about the business of setting up their own glassworks with the intent of producing paperweights of the finest quality in the style of the classics.

When the facility (set up in an old abandoned schoolhouse in Crieff) was ready, the glassworkers who were helping Stuart quit Strathearn one Friday and began work at the new Perthshire Paperweights factory on Monday morning. First, they constructed a furnace to melt glass. After completing the project in the summer of 1968, they produced their first paperweight in August, 1968.

The factory concentrated on producing what Stuart referred to as "bread and butter" weights: simple designs which could be easily sold in the local gift stores. Income from the sale of these weights allowed the workers to take some time to advance their skills and produce more complex weights. In 1969, A.G. Tillman (Antiques) Ltd. commissioned the factory to produce a limited edition red, white and blue crown. The success of this edition allowed Perthshire to produce two Annual Collection weights in 1970 and a tradition began.

Perthshire's production increased until they simply outgrew their facilities in 1970. Stuart purchased land on the outskirts of Crieff to build a new factory. The current factory is still at that location.

Perthshire Today

Over the years the site grew to include a gift shop and a restaurant and it is now known as "Crieff Visitor Centre." Buses loaded with tourists frequent the site every week. Since the death of Stuart Drysdale in 1990, Perthshire Paperweights has continued to prosper under the direction of his son, Neil.

Inside the factory, visitors will find a large viewing gallery with nothing but a very low wall between themselves and the glassblowers who work only a few feet away. This gives the visitor a very close view of hot glass being formed into paperweights. In a nearby room with a large window, a worker makes millefiori setups under the watchful eyes of visitors. Through yet another window, the skillful glass cutters can be seen working at their wheels. The gift shop has most of the factory's production weights for sale including a number of one-of-a-kind weights. However, no seconds are ever sold.

The Perthshire Paperweights factory located in Crieff, Scotland

From Sand to Art

Glass is the main component from which paperweights are made. While some paperweight makers buy their clear glass already made, Perthshire Paperweights makes its own clear glass every week. A special room is used to store a mountain of sand and the various chemicals that are added to the sand during the melting process. This room holds up to 15 tons of sand and is refilled four times a year.

The "sand" room

The factory's three furnaces are loaded with sand and chemicals every Saturday, and the melting process begins. Each furnace holds about 700 pounds of glass. By Monday morning, all three furnaces are ready to support another week of the factory's production.

The furnaces are practically empty by Friday afternoon. Weights that did not meet Perthshire's high quality standards are tossed onto the heap of glass behind the factory and covered with the small amounts of molten glass remaining in each of the furnaces. The rejected weights shatter, eliminating the possibility of the factory ever offering a "second" for sale.

Destroying rejected weights

To make the colors used in paperweights, colored glass is purchased in the form of rods about an inch or two in diameter and 12 to 18 inches long.

Color rods

The color in these rods is very concentrated so it takes only a small amount mixed with the factory's clear glass to make the desired color.

Millefiori Canes

Precise millefiori canes are one of the most recognizable features in a Perthshire paperweight. Over the years Perthshire has achieved a level of detail and complexity that is unmatched anywhere.

Cane molds

Metal molds in various shapes are used in the first step of the cane making process. A metal rod, or punty, is used to obtain a gather of glass, which is first rolled in some powdered white glass and then in some powdered colored glass. This gather is then pressed into one of the molds until it cools enough to retain the mold's shape. The shaped gather is then returned to the furnace, where a layer of clear glass is collected over the shaped glass. This is rolled in more powdered white glass and then in more colored glass until the desired shade is achieved. The gather is then pressed into a mold again. The process may be repeated several more times.

When the glassworker is satisfied with the number of layers in the cane, a punty is attached to the other end of the glass, and the gather is pulled until its diameter is reduced to 1/4 inch or less. At this

point the pull may be 20 to 30 feet long and is what is known as a simple cane.

Pulling a cane

After it cools, the simple cane is cut into pieces 6 to 10 inches long. Some of these lengths are then cut into very short pieces, about 1/8 inch long, using a diamond saw. These short pieces are the basic components in many of the millefiori weights. The longer pieces are bundled together with many other canes. The bundle is held together by a wrap of wire around each end. Reheating the bundle fuses the canes together into one large cane. The wires are removed, a punty is attached to each end, and the cane is again pulled to reduce its diameter. This produces a complex cane.

Bundles of canes ready for reheating

A complex cane can very often contain more than 50 simple canes with all the details of the original canes still visible.

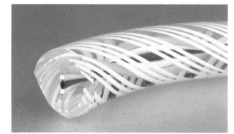

The end of a twist showing its makeup

Sometimes colored rods are heated side by side on the end of a punty and then inserted into a gather of clear glass. After rolling the outside of the gather on a clean steel plate to make it smooth and round, one end of the glass is attached to a mechanism which allows the glass to be rotated with a hand crank. The other end is then pulled while the glass is rotated, causing the rods to twist within the molten glass.

Twisting a cane

The resulting twists are often used to outline groups of millefiori canes within a design. This process is also used to make latticinio rods.

Twists and latticinio

Picture Canes

Perthshire has also perfected a technique for making picture canes. A design for a picture is drawn in color on a flat piece of clay. Hundreds of thin glass rods are painstakingly stacked side by side by pushing one end into the clay. By matching the color of the rods to the color on the clay, the design on the clay is transferred to the bundle of rods. The bundle will be several inches in diameter and may take up to four days to "build." After the bundle is complete, it is wrapped with wire and fused together in an oven.

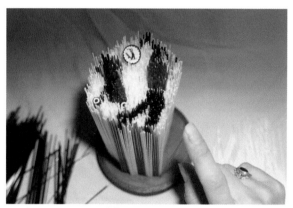

Assembling a picture cane

The finished picture cane is very often wrapped with millefiori canes and again fused. This gives the picture cane a defining border. Picture canes must be heated and pulled slowly and carefully because the various colors used in making the picture don't all melt at exactly the same temperature. After pulling, usually only a few feet of a picture cane will be usable.

Finished picture canes

Lampworking

Another process used in creating some of the basic parts of a paperweight is lampworking. A glassworker uses a small gas flame to soften and manipulate tiny glass rods of various colors and sizes. Rod shapes are changed, colors and textures are applied, and small pieces are assembled into larger ones: flowers, leaves, stems, snakes, butterflies; you name it. Just about anything can be made by the experienced lampworker.

Lampwork setups awaiting encasement

The butterfly shown being made was part of a 1995F weight.

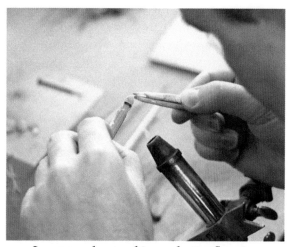

*Lampworker making a butterfly wing
from a special cane with a colored overlay*

In many cases, the lampworker needs special canes to make the needed pieces. Although some lampworkers must make their own special canes, at Perthshire these can easily be made in long lengths by the excellent millefiori cane makers on the main factory floor.

The individual pieces are assembled into completed setups and are carefully placed on sheets awaiting final encasement on the factory floor. A light tissue is placed over the finished pieces to keep dirt or dust from contaminating the lampwork. Any contamination could cause bubbles in the finished weight.

Careful examination of the bouquet setups and the bouquet in the weight shows that the setups have been laid out upside down. This is because the weight is actually made upside down. While some makers "pick up" the setup from the top, Perthshire picks it up from the bottom.

Weight Making

After all of the component parts for a paperweight have been made, they must be assembled into a finished weight. Since the exact process is different for each type of weight, general descriptions of the steps are given.

If the design includes millefiori canes, a worker, using tweezers, carefully places each cane in the proper position on a round metal plate. It is important to remember that, since the weight will be assembled from the bottom, the canes must be placed on the plate with the top of the design down. A number of setups for a single design are done at one time.

For designs in which colors vary, the worker placing the canes has complete freedom in choosing the colors. This means that, unless a design requires the weights to be identical in color, it is quite possible that no two weights will ever be exactly alike.

Assembling the millefiori setups

When the setups are complete, they are gently carried out to the factory floor where they are placed, one at a time, over a gas flame. This slowly heats the canes so that they will not crack when touched by molten glass.

A setup ready for encasement

If the design is to have a colored ground under the canes, the glass worker first gets a gather of clear glass from the fur-

nace. The hot glass is rolled in a mound of powdered (or chipped) colored glass. The glass is then reheated to melt the powder. After rolling the glass on a clean sheet of steel to give it the proper shape, it is again rolled in the powder. The process is repeated several times until the desired color is achieved. The glass is then shaped on the steel plate until it is the same size as the design to be picked up. It is then pressed down onto the cane setup for a few seconds to fuse the canes to the colored ground. When the gather is lifted, all of the canes come with it (most of the time).

Rolling the hot glass to shape it

Pressing the picked-up design onto the steel plate flattens it. The glassworker then plunges the design back into the glass furnace to pick up enough clear glass to form the dome. With the weight still attached to the punty, special tools are used to prepare the bottom of the weight and to smooth the dome until all lines are gone. For most weights, the dome finish which the glassworker achieves when the weight is hot is the same finish that is on the completed weight. It is rare that a dome is ever polished.

The same process is used if the design contains lampwork, except much more care must be taken to make sure that the delicate lampwork assembly is not broken or distorted when the hot glass is applied and that no air bubbles are trapped.

Many designs contain both canes and lampwork. In most cases the two are picked up at the same time. Occasionally, the design will have different levels within the weight. Each level is picked up separately with a thin coating of glass applied to provide separation between the layers.

Sometimes a weight has an overlay (or two, or three). While the weight is kept hot, an overlay cup is made by another glassworker. After being shaped into a cup, the overlay is placed over the weight. The cup is then sealed onto the weight, completely covering the internal design. If the design calls for them, more overlay layers are applied. Only when the facets are cut later, will the maker know if the internal design survived the process.

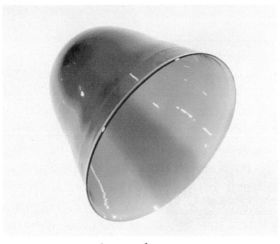

An overlay cup

When the hot process is finished, the weight is removed from the punty by holding the weight over a bucket of sand and lightly rapping on the punty until the weight breaks off. If a signature/date cane is required in the base, the bottom of the weight is heated with a torch until the cane can be pushed into the glass.

Placing a signature/date cane in the bottom of a weight

The weight is then placed in an annealing oven, which will slowly lower the temperature until it reaches room temperature. It takes at least 24 hours before the weight can be handled.

The next step is to remove the roughness caused by the punty from the bottom of the weight and to cut facets, if necessary. Six separate steps involving different wheels are necessary just to polish the bottom of a weight. If the weight has an overlay, the top facet is cut first to see which way the internal design points and to check for flaws. Some of the fancy-cut overlays may take several days or even a week to finish.

One item unique to Perthshire is their double overlay encased double overlay, or "double-double," as it is called. To make one of these, first a double overlay weight is made. The overlay is fancy-cut and finished. The weight is then placed back in an oven and heated to working temperature. A punty is reattached to the bottom and another layer of clear glass from the furnace is applied. Another set of overlays is made and placed on the

weight. It then goes back into the annealing oven and then to the faceting room
for another week of cutting. At any step
along the way, the slightest mistake can
ruin the weight. Only a very few double-
doubles are produced each year.

Head Craftsman, Peter McDougall, at work

Getting a gather of clear glass from a furnace

Pressing the gather into a mold to make a cane

Finishing the dome

Placing a weight in an annealing oven

Finishing the bottom of a weight

13

Catalogue

Perthshire classifies paperweights into three categories - Annual Collection, Limited Edition and General Range. In this book, the Limited Edition and General Range weights have been placed in a single category because they share the numbering system assigned by the factory (PP1, PP2, PP3, etc.). "PP" stands for Perthshire Paperweights and the number indicates the design.

This book also has sections for items not shown in Perthshire's yearly catalogues. These include Christmas weights, special editions, one-of-a-kind paperweights, and paperweight-related items.

The Identification Chapter shows signatures and includes other information useful in identifying specific Perthshire paperweights.

Annual Collection Weights

Each year Perthshire designs and produces limited editions of a small number of weights designated as the Annual Collection. These weights are usually lampwork or a combination of lampwork and millefiori, but a few exceptions are millefiori alone. Most of the Annual Collection weights are signed and dated.

These weights are arranged by year and include all of the designs designated as part of the Annual Collection in each year from 1969 through 1997. The weights have designations of "A," "B," "C," etc. Perthshire did not assign letter designation to the Annual Collection weights until 1983. In this book, letter designations for weights prior to 1983 are specified in the same order that they have been shown in previous publications.

Since 1983 Perthshire has designated the Annual Collection weight with the least expensive issue price with the letter, "A" and the most expensive one with the letter, "G." However, the letters between "A" and "G" have not necessarily been assigned in sequence with increasing issue price.

The present day values of the Annual Collection weights in the secondary market are based on desirability in the eyes of the collectors. It is impossible to predict which weights will become the most sought after because of changing popularity of various themes and types of work. In fact, the values of some "A" weights issued in the 1980s now exceed the values of weights from the same years with higher issue prices.

1977 Annual Collection

Christmas Weights

Since 1971, with the exception of 1973, Perthshire has created a special, limited edition Christmas design each year. All are signed and most are dated.

15

Limited Edition and General Range Weights

These weights, which have "PP" number designations, are nearly all millefiori.

General Range weights, such as the PP1, PP2, and PP3, were made over a number of years and are usually signed with a "P" cane, but not dated. Limited Edition weights, which are usually signed and dated, were made only in specific years and in specific edition sizes for each of those years. Examples of these include the PP67, PP100, and PP155. The PP14 is an example of a design produced over many years with a defined edition size each year.

Certain weights underwent design changes from year to year, without changing the PP designation. For example, the PP19 weight is always a scramble, but the appearance changed markedly in 1988. The PP12 and PP13 weights not only underwent design changes, but a specific combination of date and ground or lace color is the only way to separate the PP12s from the PP13s. The Identification Chapter has a chart showing the colors for PP12 and PP13 weights for the years in which they were made.

PP63s

Years in which design changes occurred for specific model numbers can be found in a chart in the Identification Chapter. PP32 and PP63 are designs that changed every year in which they were made. While this may sound confusing, their physical characteristics (size, millefiori and twist components, and faceting) make identification quite easy.

Double Overlay Encased Double Overlays

Special Editions

Several designs were produced as Special Editions of various sizes. Some of these were made to commemorate a specific event such as a royal wedding, the French Revolution, the Spanish Armada or the Ryder Cup. Some were made for a specific customer, such as the "Swan Boat" design that was made for a Boston jewelry store. ("Swan Boats" are a tourist attraction that operates on a pond in the Boston Gardens.) Specific designs were made for the Bergstrom-Mahler Museum and the Smithsonian Institution.

Sometimes one-of-a-kind designs are made in a series, where no two weights have the same cutting or color combinations, but the general design concept is a common thread. The Double Overlay Encased Double Overlay and the Crystal-encased Double Overlay are examples. They may or may not be dated, but all are signed.

Corporate logo weight

The items described in this book were made specifically with the collector in mind. Other small editions of items such as corporate logo weights were made by special order for various customers.

One-of-a-kind Weights

Over the years Perthshire has produced many one-of-a-kind ("one-off") weights. These include unique, one-of-a-kind de-

Prototype

1982H

Prototype

PP80

signs, prototype designs that were not produced in editions, and derivatives of produced designs. Some dishes, bowls and ashtrays are examples of items that were "derived' from regular production designs, but were not issued as designated pieces. While one-of-a-kind items are usually signed and sometimes dated, it is certainly possible to find unique pieces that can be identified only by their Perthshire characteristics.

Certificates and Boxes

Each Perthshire paperweight, with the exception of General Range weights, is issued with a certificate and a presentation box. The certificate indicates such information as issue size, the specific number of that particular weight in the edition, and the year of issue.

Perthshire boxes and certificates

Over time, the design of the presentation boxes has changed considerably and some collectors prize the original box and certificate. However, most weights in the secondary market are no longer paired with their certificate and box. Unlike with other collectibles, the presence or absence of these items does not affect the value of the weight.

Annual Collection

CROWN
Red and blue twist ribbons alternating with white latticinio rods to form a crown topped with a red, white, and blue millefiori cane. Signed "P1969" in canes in the base. This weight was specially commissioned by A. G. Tillman (Antiques) Ltd. Edition size: 350/268 made.

1969A

DRAGONFLY
A lampwork dragonfly with latticinio wings surrounded by a garland of millefiori canes on a clear ground. Cane and dragonfly colors vary. Scratch-signed "P1970" on the base. Edition size: 500/500 made.

1970A

Dark green

1970B

Dark blue

FLASH OVERLAY
A pattern of five florets set around a central floret on a clear ground within a flash overlay. Overlay colors are amethyst, ruby, dark blue, light blue, dark green, and light green. Millefiori colors vary. One top facet, five large side facets, ten small side facets, and a star-cut base. Scratch-signed "1970," "P," "AM," and "JA" on the base. The initials are for Anton Moravec and Jack Allan, craftsmen. First overlaid weight by Perthshire. Edition size: 150/150 made. (Edition size by color: amethyst - 28; ruby - 30; dark blue - 29; light blue - 20; dark green - 25; light green - 18)

1971A

OVERLAY BOTTLE
Faceted bottle with an amethyst or blue flash overlay. The bottom of the bottle has a concentric millefiori pattern and there is a single complex cane in the stopper. The bottle has twenty-four side facets and the stopper has four large and eight small facets. Signed "P1971" in canes in the base. Edition size: 300/300 made. (Edition size by color: amethyst - 147; blue - 153)

1971B

FACETED PANSY
A lampwork pansy with five leaves surrounded by a garland of millefiori canes on a white lace ground. Flower and garland colors vary. One top facet and eight side facets. Signed "P1971" in canes in the base. Edition size: 350/350 made.

CROWN
Yellow, pink, and green latticinio twists alternating with pink and white latticinio twists over a dark translucent core, meeting at a center cane that has a small flower. Signed with a "JA" cane (for Jack Allan) outlined in green in the base. Only Annual Collection weight signed by the artist and not by Perthshire. Edition size: 150/150 made.

1971C

Signature Cane Detail

CUSHION
Patterned millefiori including a pentagon formed by five latticinio rods and five canes on an opaque color ground. Colors vary. Signed "P1971" in canes in the base. Edition size: 250/250 made.

1971D

PINK DAHLIA
A dahlia consisting of four layers of pink lampwork petals. One top facet and four side facets. Signed "P1972" in canes in the base. Edition size: 200/200 made.

1972A

FACETED CUSHION
Patterned millefiori including five latticinio rods and five canes which form a pentagon. Colors vary. Identical to the 1971D Cushion except for one top facet and ten side facets. Signed "P1972" in canes in the base. Edition size: 300/300 made.

1972B

MINIATURE FLOWER

1972C

Small lampwork flower floating inside a stave basket. Flower and basket colors vary. Signed "P" in the center of the flower. Perthshire's first use of a stave basket. Edition size: 1000/1000 made.

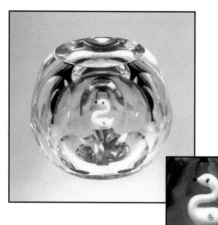

SWAN IN THE POND

1973A

A hollow weight with a lampwork swan sitting on a light green pond. One top facet, sixteen side facets and a star-cut base. Unsigned, or signed "P" on the wing of the swan. Perthshire's first hollow weight. Edition size: 250/250 made.

CLEMATIS FLOWER ON A BASKET

1973B

An amethyst clematis with five twisted petals, six green leaves, and a stem on a white double spiral latticinio cushion. The edges of each flower petal are highlighted in blue and white. Signed "P" in the center of the flower. Perthshire's first use of double spiral latticinio. Edition size: 300/300 made.

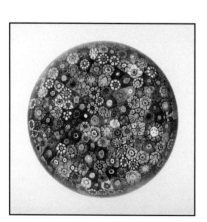

CLOSEPACKED MILLEFIORI

1973C

A closepacked millefiori design using complex canes on an opaque purple ground. Signed "P1973" in a cane within the design. Edition size: 400/378 made.

FACETED CARPET GROUND
Five black and white silhouette or picture canes on a white carpet ground over a translucent amethyst ground. One top facet and five side facets. Signed "P1973" in a separate cane within the design. First use of silhouette canes and picture canes in an Annual Collection weight. Edition size: 350/348 made.

1973D

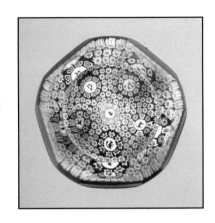

MINIATURE FLOWER
A five-petaled flower with two leaves and a stem on a clear ground. One top facet, eight side facets, and a grid-cut base. Flower colors vary. Signed "P" in the center of the flower. Perthshire's first use of a grid-cut base. Edition size: 600/563 made.

1973E

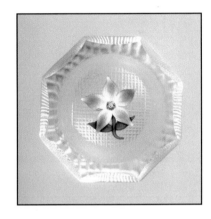

SPACED MILLEFIORI
A center cane surrounded by a ring of six spaced canes and then by a ring of twelve spaced canes, all on a translucent blue ground. Signed "P1974" in a cane within the design. Edition size: 500/425 made.

1974A

FLOWER AND BUDS
A white flower with six dark-tipped petals on a stem with two buds on an opaque lilac ground. Signed "P" in a cane beside the base of the stem. Edition size: 350/345 made.

1974B

23

1974C

BOUQUET & DRAGONFLY
Bouquet of a pansy and two clematis flowers with a hovering lampwork dragonfly that has white latticinio wings. The bouquet is tied with a yellow ribbon and is set on a clear ground. One top facet, five side facets, and a grid-cut base. Signed "P" in the center of the pansy. Edition size: 300/300 made.

1974D

GARLAND
A patterned millefiori design arranged in four quadrants and centered around a colored picture cane of a flower on an opaque color ground. Ground and cane colors vary. Signed with a "P1974" cane in the base. First Annual Collection weight with a colored picture cane. Edition size: 350/334 made.

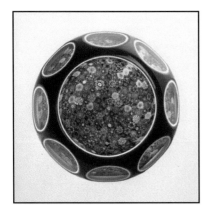

1974E

DOUBLE OVERLAY
A closepacked millefiori design on an opaque amethyst cushion within a double overlay with purple and white. One top facet and sixteen side facets. Signed "P1974" in a cane within the design. Perthshire's first double overlay. Edition size: 300/300 made.

1975A

TUDOR ROSE
A lampwork four-petaled rose with a circular stem and leaves surrounded by a ring of eight spaced millefiori canes on a translucent blue ground. Signed "P1975" in canes in the base and "P" in the center of the rose. Edition size: 400/400 made.

PENGUIN

A penguin on an ice floe inside a hollow weight with a pale blue flash overlay. One top facet and sixteen side facets. Signed "P" in the base of the ice floe. Edition size: 350/316 made.

1975B

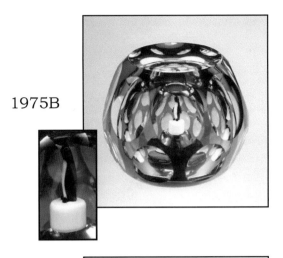

MILLEFIORI CIRCLETS

A center millefiori cluster surrounded by five spaced millefiori clusters, all surrounded by a ring of canes and set on an opaque color ground. Cane and ground colors vary. Signed "P" in the center of the design. Edition size: 400/400 made.

1975C

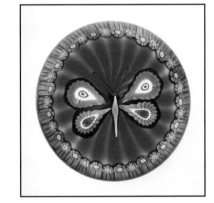

BUTTERFLY

A large butterfly with millefiori wings surrounded by a garland of millefiori canes on a ribbed opaque colored cushion ground. Butterfly, cane and ground colors vary. Signed with a "P1975" cane in the base. Edition size: 450/372 made.

1975D

OVERLAY BOTTLE

A tall bottle with a flash overlay of blue or green and a concentric millefiori pattern in the base. The bottle has twenty-four side facets. The stopper has a matching flash overlay, eight side facets, and a single cane at the top, which matches the center of the concentric pattern in the bottle. Signed with a "P1975" cane in the base. Edition size: 350/347 made.

1975E

1976A

FORGET-ME-NOT
A nosegay of four light blue florets with two stems and four leaves on a pale yellow-green double spiral latticinio cushion. Signed with a "P1976" cane in the base. Perthshire's first colored latticinio cushion. Edition size: 400/397 made.

1976B

MINIATURE OVERLAY BUTTERFLY
A lampwork butterfly with stretched millefiori wings floating within a miniature double overlay with unusual spiraling side cuts. Overlay colors are red, blue, or green over white. Butterfly colors vary. Signed with a "P" cane under one wing. Edition size: 500/488 made.

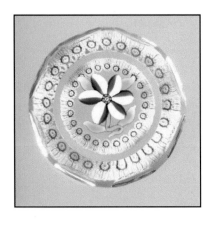

1976C

MINIATURE FACETED FLOWER
A flower with six blue and white striped petals, a stem, and four leaves surrounded by a garland of pink millefiori canes. One top facet and eight side facets. Signed "P" in the center of the flower. Edition size: 400/369 made.

1976D

MAGNUM CUSHION
A hexagonal pattern of latticinio rods and millefiori canes on a raised cushion with a window through which a closepacked millefiori design on a lower level can be seen. One top facet. Signed with a "P1976" cane in the base. First use of a two-layer design, where the bottom layer is visible only through an opening in the top layer. This design appears to be unique to Perthshire. Edition size: 300/295 made.

MOSS GROUND
A complex center cane surrounded by three concentric rings of green moss canes alternating with two rings of red and white canes. Signed with a "P1976" cane in the base. Edition size: 300/168 made.

1976E

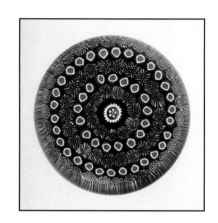

MINIATURE NOSEGAY
Three florets, one red, one blue, and one yellow, four green leaves, and a stem and set on a latticinio cushion made with alternating bands of pink and green threads. Signed with a "P" cane in the flat base. Edition size: 400/315 made.

1977A

PLUMS
A miniature weight with three plums with stems and three leaves on clear ground. One top facet, sixteen side facets, and a grid-cut base. Scratch-signed "P" on a small facet near the base. Edition size: 500/315 made.

1977B

TRIPLE OVERLAY
A triple overlay of yellow over white over pink encasing a white lampwork flower with four leaves. One top facet, sixteen side facets, and a star-cut base. Signed with a "P" in the center of the flower. Perthshire's first triple overlay. Edition size: 400/347 made.

1977C

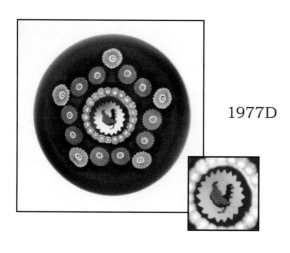

1977D

ROOSTER
An opaque red cushion ground with a window through which a large colored picture cane of a rooster can be seen. Signed with a "P1977" cane in the base. Edition size: 350/334 made.

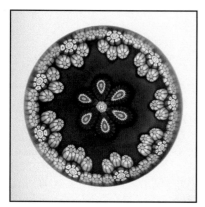

1977E

PATTERNED MILLEFIORI
Six petal-shaped canes arranged around a center cane to form a flower which is surrounded by a scalloped garland on a translucent color ground. Colors vary. Signed with a "P" in the center of the flower. Edition size: 400/346 made.

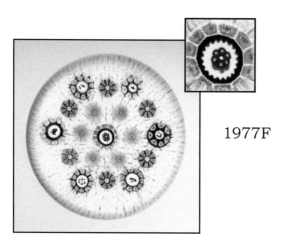

1977F

CARPET GROUND
A central colored picture cane of a flower surrounded by a ring of six spaced millefiori canes and then by a ring of six spaced colored picture canes alternating with six millefiori canes on a carpet of pale yellow millefiori canes with green centers. The picture canes are of various flowers, birds, and animals. Signed with a "P1977" cane in the base. Edition size: 400/338 made.

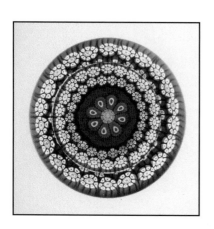

1978A

PATTERNED MILLEFIORI
A central millefiori cane surrounded by a ring of eight petal-shaped canes and two rings of millefiori canes on a translucent color ground. Cane and ground colors vary. One top facet. Signed with a "P1978" cane in the base. Edition size: 350/292 made.

28

HEATHER

A Scottish heather sprig surrounded by a ring of alternating amethyst and green millefiori canes on a translucent blue ground. Signed with a "P1978" cane in the base. Edition size: 500/452 made.

1978B

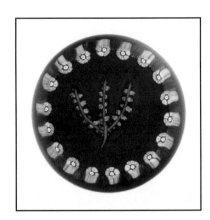

BLUEBELL

Three Scottish bluebell blossoms on a stem with green leaves. One top facet, sixteen side facets, and a star-cut base. Signed "P" in a cane beside the stem. Edition size: 350/350 made.

1978C

BOUQUET

A bouquet of three lampwork flowers and a bud connected by a dark green stem on a black ground. Flower colors vary. Signed "P" in the center of a flower. Edition size: 350/350 made.

1978D

DOUBLE OVERLAY

An interlaced garland with six loops encircling six colored picture canes on an opaque blue ground within a double overlay of blue over white. One top facet and twelve side facets. Signed "P" in the center cane. Some also signed with a "JD" cane (for John Deacons) in the base. Edition size: 250/119 made.

1978E

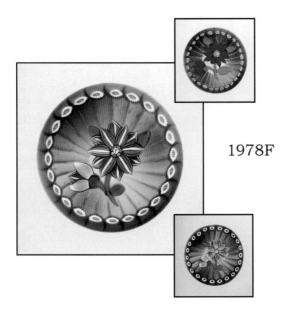

1978F

MINIATURE CLEMATIS
A red, pink or yellow double clematis and bud floating above a stave basket. Basket colors vary. Signed with a "P" in the center of the flower. Edition size: 400/374 made.

1979A

SUNFLOWER
A gold lampwork sunflower with a garland of green leaves and an outer ring of spaced millefiori canes on a burnt umber ground. Signed with a "P1979" cane in the base. Edition size: 350/303 made.

1979B

BLUE SILHOUETTE
A center millefiori cane surrounded by close concentric rings of millefiori canes and four silhouette canes that are in the corners of a square of twists, all on a translucent blue ground. One top facet and eight side facets. Signed with a "P1979" cane in the base. Edition size: 450/373 made.

1979C

MINIATURE OVERLAY
An upright six-petaled flower and leaves within a double overlay of blue over white. One top facet, eight side facets, and a grid-cut base. Signed with a "P" in the center of the flower. Edition size: 400/351 made.

GARLAND

A central colored picture cane surrounded by a garland with six loops, each encircling a colored picture cane, all on an opaque ruby ground. Garland colors vary. Signed with a "P1979" cane in the base. Edition size: 400/293 made.

1979D

SEAL

A seal perched on a spiral-striped stand, balancing a ball on its nose within a hollow weight with a ruby flash overlay. One top facet and sixteen side facets. Signed "P" in the base of the seal's stand. Edition size: 400/275 made.

1979E

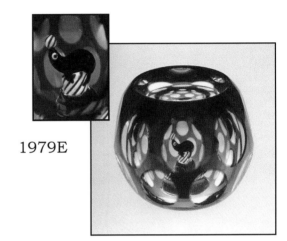

OVERLAY BOTTLE

Bottle with a blue or amber flash overlay, faceted to reveal a lampwork flower in the bottom. The stopper has a matching bud. The bottle has twenty-four side facets and the stopper has sixteen side facets. Signed "P" in the center of the flower in the bottom of the bottle. Edition size: 500/331 made.

1979F

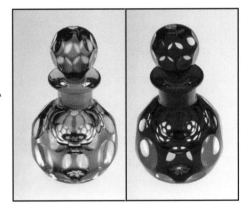

BOUQUET

Five lampwork flowers arranged in a bouquet on a clear ground. Flower colors vary. One top facet, sixteen side facets, and a star-cut base. Signed with a "P" cane beside the bouquet. Edition size: 450/332 made.

1979G

ROSE AND BUD

1980A

A pink lampwork rose and bud with green leaves and stem on a clear ground. One top facet, sixteen side facets, and a star-cut base. Signed with a "P" cane beside the rose stem. Edition size: 300/224 made.

OVERLAY ROSE

1980B

A pink lampwork rose and large bud on a clear ground within an apple-green flash overlay. One top facet, sixteen side facets, and a star-cut base. Signed with a "P" cane beside the rose stem. Edition size: 200/167 made.

FLORAL OVERLAY

1980C

A blue lampwork flower surrounded by a garland of three red and three white buds, all on a translucent dark amethyst cushion ground within an amethyst flash overlay. One top facet and twelve side facets with six flutes around the base. Signed with a "P" in the center of the flower. Edition size: 300/212 made.

FRUIT

1980D

A pear, an orange, a lemon, and three cherries on a bed of leaves, all on a single spiral latticinio ground. Signed with a "P1980" cane in the base. Patterned in the style of antique St. Louis fruit weights. Edition size: 350/228 made.

TRIPLE SWIRL

A three-color swirl with a complex millefiori cane in the center. Colors vary. Signed with a "P1980" cane in the base. While most of these were made with the swirl going counterclockwise toward the center (as pictured), three were made going in the opposite (clockwise) direction. Edition size: 300/244 made.

1980E

MINIATURE FLOWER

A central sunflower surrounded by five small nosegays, each with three florets and two leaves, all on an opaque ruby or blue ground. Signed with a "P1980" cane in the base. Edition size: 450/357 made.

1980F

TRANSPORTATION GARLAND

A central complex cane and five colored picture canes, each representing a form of old-time transportation, in a looped garland, all on a white lace ground. Each loop of the garland is a different color. Garland colors vary. Signed with a "P1980" cane in the base. Edition size: 400/285 made.

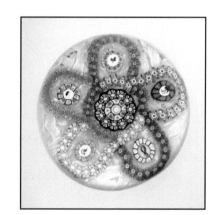

1980G

SAILING BOAT

A central colored picture cane of a sail boat on blue water surrounded by rings of canes and pairs of millefiori twists, all set above two layers of latticinio strips set at 90 degrees to one another. Cane colors vary. Signed with a "P1980" cane in the base. Edition size: 300/189 made.

1980H

1980I

FISH
Three tropical fish swimming amidst blue-green seaweed over a seabed. One top facet and twelve side facets. Fish colors and seabed contents and colors vary. Signed with a "P1980" cane in the base. Edition size: 400/400 made.

1981A

MINIATURE SWIRL
A six-petaled pink flower with three pairs of green leaves on white single spiral latticinio over a honey-amber ground. Signed with a "P1981" cane in the base. Edition size: 350/264 made.

1981B

FLOWER AND MILLEFIORI
A lampwork flower surrounded by four rings of millefiori canes that are divided into panels by millefiori twists, all on a translucent color ground. Colors vary. Signed with a "P1981" cane in the base. Edition size: 250/222 made.

1981C

AQUARIUM
A seahorse, a crab, a snail and two fish amidst pink seaweed over a grey sand ground. One top facet and twenty-four side facets. Animal colors vary. Signed with a "P1981" cane in the base. Edition size: 350/237 made.

BLUE GENTIAN

A blue lampwork flower with a complex center cane on parallel white latticinio strips, above a blue cushion, all encircled by an outer ring of blue millefiori canes that are pulled down to form a basket. Signed with a "P1981" cane in the base. Edition size: 400/265 made.

1981D

ACORNS

Two acorns with oak leaves on a white single spiral latticinio ground. One top facet, eight side facets, and twenty-four small oval facets. Signed with a "P1981" cane in the base. Edition size: 300/236 made.

1981E

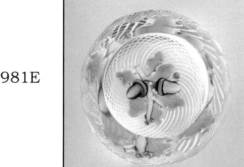

CROWN WEIGHT

A pink or yellow lampwork flower with green leaves on a single spiral latticinio cushion surrounded by blue-green twist spokes alternating with white latticinio rods. One top facet. Signed with a "P1981" cane in the base. Edition size: 200/193 made.

1981F

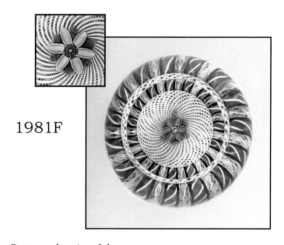

Bottom showing 3 bees

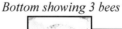

BEES

A magnum, clear, spherical weight with honeycomb faceting that causes three or four bees to appear as a swarm. Diamond-cut base. Approximately the first twenty of these weights contained three bees. The remaining weights (approximately 180) were made with four bees instead of three to make the swarm appear larger. Unsigned. Edition size: 200/200 made.

1981G

Bottom showing 4 bees

1981H

AMBER OVERLAY

Closepacked millefiori design with a double overlay of amber over white. Faceting varies and can be four-, five-, or six-sided with a flat top facet. Signed with a "P1981" cane in the base. Edition size: 250/152 made.

1982A

MILLEFIORI FLOWER

A five-petaled flower with a complex cane center surrounded by a close ring of canes and a garland of spaced canes on a translucent color ground. Cane and ground colors vary. Signed with a "P1982" cane in the base. Edition size: 300/243 made.

1982B

FLAMINGO

A pink flamingo standing on one leg in a blue pond with water lilies. One top facet. Signed with a "P1982" cane in the base. Edition size: 300/184 made.

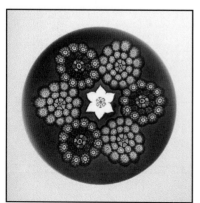

1982C

GARLAND

A white six-petaled flower surrounded by six millefiori clusters, each consisting of two rings around a central cane, all on a translucent ruby ground. Signed with a "P1982" cane in the base. Edition size: 300/165 made.

STAR PATTERN

A large eight-pointed star pattern of tiny millefiori canes on a clear ground. Colors vary. One top facet, all-over honeycomb side facets, and a star-cut base. Signed "P" in the center of the star. Edition size: 300/237 made.

1982D

NURSERY RHYME SILHOUETTES

A central millefiori cluster surrounded by five large colored picture canes depicting nursery rhyme and cartoon characters and an outer garland of canes, all on a bright blue ground. Signed with a "P1982" cane in the base. Edition size: 300/201 made.

1982E

SPRAY

Five pale pink lampwork flowers with buds and leaves on a translucent pale blue ground. One top facet with all-over honeycomb side facets. Signed with a "P" cane next to the design. Edition size: 300/141 made.

1982F

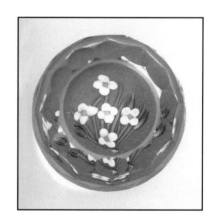

POMPON

A large deep-pink flower and bud, formed from a honeycomb cane, with a green stem and leaves on a translucent ruby ground. Ruby flash overlay with one top facet, twelve side facets, and six scalloped facets around the top. Signed with a "P1982" cane in the base. Edition size: 300/215 made.

1982G

1982H

DOUBLE OVERLAY
A bouquet of three lampwork flowers and two opening buds within a double overlay of blue over white. One flat top facet, fancy-cut sides, and a star-cut base. Signed with a "P" cane at the base of the stems. Edition size: 300/205 made.

1983A

MILLEFIORI FLOWER
A yellow lampwork flower with two leaves and a stem surrounded by a square of twists, a ring of millefiori canes, and a ring of twists, all on a translucent color ground. Cane and ground colors vary. Signed with a "P1983" cane in the base. Edition size: 300/241 made.

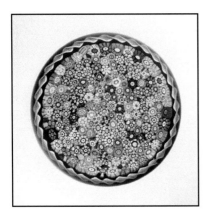

1983B

CLOSEPACKED MILLEFIORI
Closepacked millefiori canes surrounded by a torsade on an opaque dark blue ground. Signed with a "P1983" cane in the base. Edition size: 300/230 made.

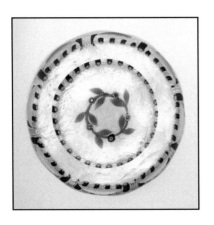

1983C

POSY RING
Five florets on a circular stem with five pairs of green leaves surrounded by a ring of alternating yellow and blue canes on a white lace ground. One top facet and twenty-eight side facets. Signed with a "P1983" cane in the base. Edition size: 300/187 made.

CARPET GROUND

A blue lampwork flower encircled by two rings of spaced millefiori canes on a carpet of pink canes on an opaque pink ground. Signed with a "P1983" cane in the base. Edition size: 300/141 made.

1983D

BOUQUET

Two lampwork flowers and a complex cane flower resembling a Clichy-type rose in a bouquet surrounded by two rings of millefiori canes, all on a clear ground. One top facet, five side facets, and a grid-cut base. Signed with a "P" cane in the outer ring of canes. Edition size: 300/194 made.

1983E

WATER LILY

A small lampwork butterfly sitting atop a pink water lily with two buds and three leaves on a translucent multicolored ground. One top facet and ten side facets. Signed with a "P1983" cane in the base. Edition size: 300/205 made.

1983F

DUCKS IN THE POND

Three ducks sitting on a blue-green pond in a hollow weight with a light green flash overlay. One top facet and sixteen side facets. Signed with a "P1983" cane in the base. Edition size: 300/254 made.

1983G

1984A

FLOWER POT
Three pink flowers in a pot surrounded by a crescent of spaced millefiori canes, all on an opaque blue ground. Signed with a "P1984" cane in the base. Edition size: 300/124 made.

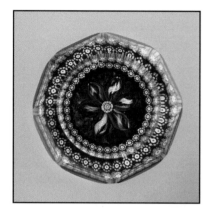

1984B

MILLEFIORI PETAL
Large flower with six latticinio-twist petals outlined in color surrounded by two rings of canes on a translucent color ground. Colors vary. One top facet and eight side facets. Signed with a "P1984" cane in the base. Edition size: 300/221 made.

1984C

CATERPILLAR
A green caterpillar and two green leaves on a clear ground. The caterpillar is made of horizontal millefiori cane segments set side by side such that the exposed ends form the black spots on the sides of the caterpillar. One top facet and twenty side finger facets. Signed "P" in a cane under one leaf. Edition size: 300/208 made.

1984D

FLORAL SPRAY
A large pink or blue lampwork flower with four or five buds on a white double spiral latticinio cushion. Signed with a "P" cane in the base. Edition size: 400/271 made.

CROWN
A yellow lampwork flower with leaves on a crown of gold aventurine and yellow and white twists over a translucent blue core. Signed with a "P1984" cane in the base. Perthshire's first use of aventurine. Edition size: 300/152 made.

1984E

SQUIRREL
A squirrel sitting on a branch in a hollow weight with an amber flash overlay. One top facet with four oval and four long side facets. Signed with a "P1984" cane in the base. This was the smallest production (94) for any Annual Collection weight. Edition size: 200/94 made.

1984F

DOUBLE OVERLAY
A pink flower and two buds on a single spiral latticinio cushion within a double overlay of ruby over white. One top facet and twenty-four side facets. Signed with a "P" cane in the base. Edition size: 300/288 made.

1984G

MINIATURE FLOWER
A miniature weight containing a pink or blue flower with green leaves on a double spiral latticinio cushion. Signed with a "P" cane in the base. Edition size: 400/292 made.

1985A

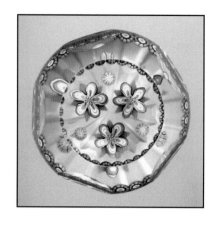

1985B

FACETED PRIMROSES
Three pink and white flowers and three spaced canes surrounded by a millefiori cane garland on a clear ground. Cane colors vary. One top facet, five side facets, and a star-cut base. Signed with a "P" cane in the garland. Edition size: 250/177 made.

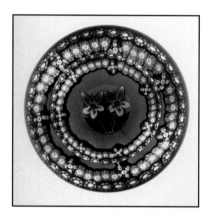

1985C

WILD PANSIES
Two wild pansies and three leaves surrounded by a double garland of millefiori canes on a translucent blue, ruby, green, or amethyst ground. Cane colors vary. One top facet. Signed with a "P" cane in the base. Edition size: 350/337 made.

1985D

DAHLIA BLOSSOM
An upright pink and white dahlia blossom above two layers of green leaves on a clear ground. One top facet and twelve side finger facets. Signed with a "P" cane in the center of the flower. Edition size: 300/156 made.

1985E

SCOTTISH BROOM
Yellow blossoms and buds on green stems over a translucent green ground. One top facet with eight large and twenty-four small side facets. Signed with a "P" cane at the base of the stems. Edition size: 350/227 made.

TRIPLE OVERLAY
Five blue-petaled flowers with white edges forming a bouquet within a triple overlay of blue over
white over pink. One top facet with six large
and twelve small side facets and a diamond-cut
base. Signed with a "P" cane at the base of the
stems. Edition size: 250/130 made.

1985F

POLAR BEAR
A polar bear and cub standing on an ice floe
in a hollow weight with a blue flash overlay.
One top facet and sixteen side facets. Signed
with a "P1985" cane in the base. Edition size:
300/282 made.

1985G

CLOSEPACKED MILLEFIORI
A closepacked millefiori pattern containing
many small complex canes on a lace ground.
Signed with a "P1986" cane in the center of the
design. Edition size: 400/379 made.

1986A

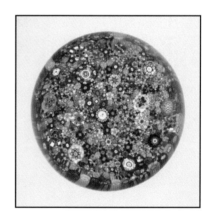

BOUQUET
A bouquet of four lampwork flowers and two
buds surrounded by a ring of twists and an
outer ring of millefiori canes on a translucent
red, green, or amethyst ground. Cane colors
vary. One top facet and six side facets. Signed
with a "P1986" cane in the base. Edition size:
300/211 made.

1986B

1986C

DRAGONFLY
A dragonfly with latticinio wings and an aventurine body perched on a leaf on a clear ground. One top facet, six large and three small side facets, and a star-cut base. Signed with a "P" cane under the branch in the design. Edition size: 300/170 made.

1986D

STRAWBERRIES
Two ripe strawberries with a central white flower, three buds, and leaves on a clear ground. One top facet, twelve side facets, and a strawberry-cut base. Signed with a "P" cane in the design. Perthshire's first use of a strawberry-cut base. Edition size: 300/218 made.

1986E

LARGE BOUQUET
Bouquet containing a large white and amber flower with "seashell ridges" on its petals, a bud, and two more flowers on an opaque deep blue ground. Signed with a "P1986" cane in the base. Edition size: 250/188 made.

1986F

DOUBLE OVERLAY MUSHROOM
A closepacked millefiori design pulled down to form a mushroom within a double overlay of green over white. One top facet with five large and five small side facets. Signed with a "P" cane in the base or in the design. Perthshire's first mushroom weight. Edition size: 250/141 made.

GOLDEN DAHLIA
Four layers of amber petals forming a large upright dahlia blossom. One top facet and five side facets. Signed with a "P" cane in the center. Edition size: 300/279 made.

1986G

FACETED BUTTERFLIES
Three small butterflies and three complex canes surrounded by a garland of canes on a clear ground. One top facet and six side facets. Signed with a "P" cane in the garland. Edition size: 300/219 made.

1987A

SNOWDROPS
A double overlay of green or red over white containing a small group of three white snowdrops. One top facet and spiral side cuts. Signed with a "P" cane at the base of the stems. Edition size: 300/294 made.

1987B

THEOBROMA CACAO FLOWER & PODS
A stylized pink and yellow flower and green pods on a clear ground. One top facet with small scalloped facets around its edge, eight side facets, and a star-cut base. Signed with a "P" cane next to the design. Edition size: 350/172 made.

1987C

1987D

HUMMINGBIRD
A hummingbird feeding from a pair of blue gentians on a clear ground. One top facet, sixteen side facets, and a deep diamond-cut base. Signed with a "P" cane beside the flower stems. Edition size: 300/160 made.

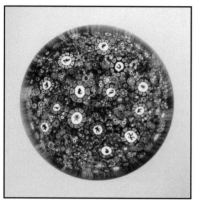

1987E

MAGNUM CLOSEPACKED MILLEFIORI
A magnum closepacked millefiori design containing many complex and picture canes on a translucent green ground. Signed with a "P1987" cane in the base. Edition size: 250/150 made.

1987F

AMERICAN BALD EAGLE
An American bald eagle perched on a rock in a hollow weight with a ruby flash overlay. One top facet and sixteen side facets. Signed with a "P1987" cane in the base. Edition size: 300/198 made.

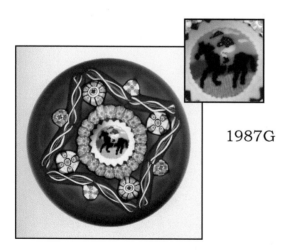

1987G

HORSE & JOCKEY MILLEFIORI
A pattern of canes and twists on an opaque blue ground with a window through which a large colored picture cane of a horse and jockey surrounded by concentric rings of canes can be seen on a lower level. A few have a single top facet. Signed with a "P1987" cane in the base. Edition size: 250/120 made.

MINIATURE BUTTERFLY

A butterfly with pink and yellow millefiori wings above a stave basket. Basket colors vary. Signed with a "P" cane in two of the wings. Edition size: 400/352 made.

1988A

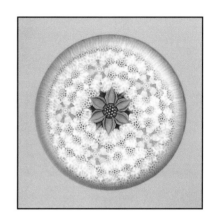

MINIATURE PATTERNED MILLEFIORI

A pink flower surrounded by five millefiori canes set on a bed of pale green and white honeycomb canes over a translucent ruby ground. Millefiori cane colors vary. Signed with a "P1988" cane in the base. Edition size: 400/254 made.

1988B

SMALL DOUBLE OVERLAY

A Scottish thistle with two flowers and leaves surrounded by three concentric rings of millefiori canes, double overlaid in green or amethyst over white. One top facet with six large and six small side facets. Signed with a "P" cane in the outer ring of canes. Edition size: 400/313 made.

1988C

APPLES

Two green apples and a white apple blossom on a branch on a translucent blue ground. One top facet and eight side facets. Signed with a "P" cane beside the branch. Edition size: 200/126 made.

1988D

1988E

BOUQUET
A bouquet of four flowers and two buds on a black swirl pattern on a translucent blue or amethyst ground. Signed with a "P1988" cane in the base. Edition size: 350/189 made.

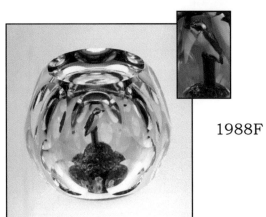

1988F

KINGFISHER
A kingfisher sitting on a stump in a hollow weight with a light green flash overlay. One top facet and sixteen side facets. Signed with a "P1988" cane in the base. Edition size: 250/139 made.

1988G

LARGE UPRIGHT FLOWER
A large upright flower with a stem and leaves above a pattern of six millefiori circles containing honeycomb canes set over a translucent ruby or green ground. One top facet and six side facets. Signed "P" in the center of the flower. Edition size: 250/185 made.

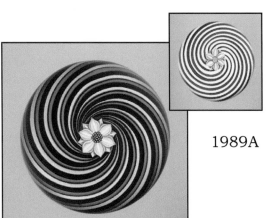

1989A

MINIATURE SWIRL
A miniature swirl weight with canes of assorted colors and a central lampwork flower. Colors of swirl and flower vary. Signed with a "P" cane in the base. Edition size: 600/591 made.

1989B

MILLEFIORI BUTTERFLY
A butterfly made entirely of millefiori canes within an outer millefiori cane garland, all on a translucent dark blue ground. Colors vary. One top facet. Signed with a "P" cane in the base. Edition size: 300/209 made.

1989C

DOUBLE OVERLAY
A three-flower lampwork bouquet within a double overlay of green or amethyst over white. One top facet, sixteen side facets, and a star-cut base. Signed with a "P" cane beside the stem. Edition size: 400/216 made.

1989D

FROG
A frog sitting on a spotted translucent cushion in a hollow weight with an amethyst flash overlay. One top facet and sixteen side facets. Signed with a "P1989" cane in the base. Edition size: 250/124 made.

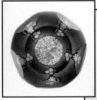

1989E

MILLEFIORI CUSHION
A closepacked millefiori design surrounded by five three-cane millefiori nosegays with green leaves and stems on an opaque ruby or turquoise cushion ground. One top facet and five side facets. Signed with a "P" cane in the base. Edition size: 200/148 made.

1989F

CHERRIES

Five red cherries with green leaves and stems on a clear ground. All-over honeycomb faceting to make the cherries appear as many more than five. Grid-cut base. Scratch-signed "P" on a facet near the base. Edition size: 300/154 made.

1989G

CLOSEPACKED MILLEFIORI

A large closepacked millefiori design of extremely complex canes, in which every cane is different. Signed "PP1989" in a cane in the center. Edition size: 300/214 made.

1990A

PATTERNED MILLEFIORI

A central group of canes surrounded by a ring of canes and then by cane groups in the form of lines and crosses, all on a translucent selenium red ground. One top facet and six side facets. Signed with a "P" cane in the base. Edition size: 300/193 made.

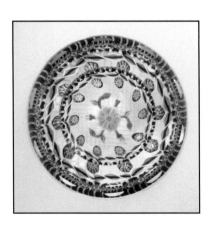

1990B

LARGE MILLEFIORI

A central lampwork flower with six radiating buds surrounded by concentric rings of spaced canes, twists and close canes. Flower and cane colors vary. One top facet, twenty side facets, and a grid-cut base. Signed with a "P" cane in the inner ring of spaced canes. Edition size: 300/249 made.

MINIATURE CROWN

Alternating white latticinio rods and blue, yellow and white twists meeting at a central millefiori pompon cane. Signed with a "P" cane in the base. Edition size: 400/224 made.

1990C

BOUQUET

A multicolored lampwork bouquet with six flowers and several buds on a black ground. One top facet and eight side facets. Signed with a "P" cane at the base of the stems. Edition size: 350/260 made.

1990D

DOUBLE OVERLAY

A lampwork butterfly, blue flower and three buds within a double overlay of ruby over white. One top facet and sixteen side facets with many tiny notch cuts around the top facet. Signed with a "P" cane at the base of the stems. Edition size: 300/132 made.

1990E

LARGE BOUQUET

A three-dimensional lampwork bouquet of six flowers and two buds on a clear ground. One top facet, eight large and sixteen tiny side facets, and a grid-cut base. Signed with a "P" cane at the base of the stems. Edition size: 300/295 made.

1990F

1990G

CLOSEPACKED MILLEFIORI PEDESTAL
A magnum piedouche with a closepacked millefiori design and vertical rows of white latticinio in the pedestal. Ten facets around pedestal foot. Signed with a "PP1990" cane in the center of the top and a "PMcD" cane (for the maker, Peter McDougall) near the outer edge. Perthshire's first pedestal weight. Edition size: 200/163 made.

1991A

BOUQUET ON BLACK
A lampwork bouquet with a large blue flower and two sprays of four yellow buds, all surrounded by alternating millefiori canes and spokes of white latticinio on a black ground. Signed with a "P1991" cane in the base. Edition size: 300/300 made.

1991B

ENCASED CLOSEPACK
A small closepacked millefiori design encased in clear crystal with twenty vertical white latticinio rods around the outside. One top facet. Signed with a "P1991" cane in the base. Edition size: 300/300 made.

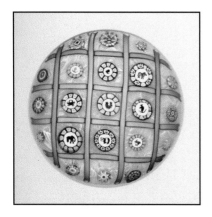

1991C

CHEQUERBOARD
A chequerboard formed by blue rods that separate picture canes in the nine center squares and twelve complex canes around the outside, all on a white lace ground. Signed with a "P1991" cane in the base. Edition size: 350/350 made.

FACETED COLUMBINE
A white flower with three pink buds surrounded by a looping millefiori garland of pink and white canes on a translucent ruby or clear ground. One top facet and eight side facets. Signed with a "P" cane at the base of the stems. Edition size: 300/234 made.

1991D

PINK AND WHITE ROSE
A pink and white rose with two buds set on a single spiral latticinio cushion above a translucent dark amethyst ground. Domed or with one top facet and six side facets. Signed with a "P1991" cane in the base. Edition size: 300/241 made.

1991E

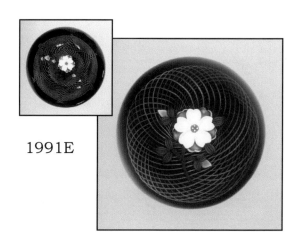

TRANSLUCENT OVERLAY
A multicolored bouquet on a clear ground within a blue flash overlay. One top facet with six large and twelve small side facets. A very deep diamond-cut on the base causes it to appear frosted. Signed with a "P" cane at the base of the stems. Edition size: 300/178 made.

1991F

THREE-DIMENSIONAL BOUQUET
A three-dimensional bouquet containing five flowers and three red berries on a clear ground. One top facet, twelve side facets, and a star-cut base. Signed with a "P" cane beside the design. Edition size: 300/170 made.

1991G

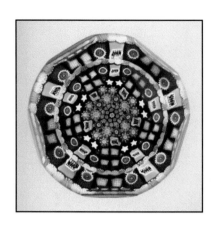

1992A

PATTERNED MILLEFIORI
A concentric patterned millefiori design containing five sets of square canes on a ruby or amethyst ground. One top facet and five side facets. Signed with a "P1992" cane in the base. Edition size: 350/350 made.

1992B

SUNFLOWER
Concentric rings of yellow and orange canes surrounded by amber and green petals forming a large sunflower on a translucent green ground. One top facet. Signed with a "P1992" cane in the base. Edition size: 350/350 made.

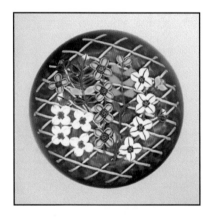

1992C

CLEMATIS ON TRELLIS
Clematis flowers of white and lavender climbing a trellis set on a translucent green ground. Signed with a "P" cane in the base. Edition size: 300/277 made.

1992D

ROSE BOUQUET
A bouquet with three upright yellow roses and two buds set on a translucent blue ground. One top facet and six side facets. Signed with a "P" cane at the base of the stems. Edition size: 300/254 made.

OVERLAY BASKET
A spray of flowers and buds on a double spiral latticinio cushion within a translucent amethyst overlay. One top facet and twelve side facets. Signed with a "P" cane at the edge of the design. Edition size: 300/300 made.

1992E

MAGNUM GARLAND
A magnum weight with a central cane cluster surrounded by a two-color double garland of five loops on a clear ground within a ruby flash overlay. One top facet, five large and ten small side facets, and a star-cut base. Some are acratch-signed with a "P" and the edition number on the basal rim, and some are signed on the base with the edition number only. Edition size: 300/160 made.

1992F

GIANT PANDA
A Giant Panda holding a green leaf in a hollow weight with a blue flash overlay. One top facet and sixteen side facets. Signed with a "P1992" cane in the base. Edition size: 300/126 made.

1992G

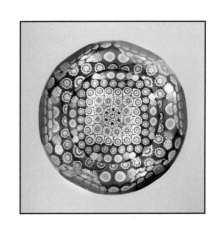

COMPLEX MILLEFIORI
Complex millefiori canes set in a square pattern on a translucent green ground. One top facet and six side facets. Signed with a "P1993" cane in the base. Edition size: 350/191 made.

1993A

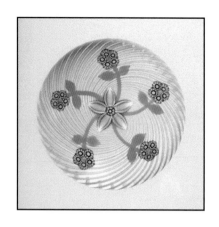

1993B

SWIRL
Five millefiori florets with stems and leaves surrounding an amber flower on a delicate blue and green single spiral latticinio ground. Signed with a "P" cane in the base. Edition size: 300/198 made.

1993C

BARBER POLE
A central complex cane surrounded by two rings of spaced canes, all separated by ruby and white latticinio rods. Cane colors vary. Signed with a "P1993" cane in the base. Edition size: 350/258 made.

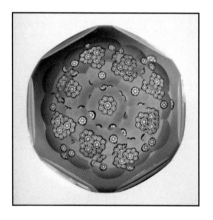

1993D

FACETED MILLEFIORI CLUSTERS
Nine clusters of small millefiori canes on a translucent blue translucent ground. Honeycomb top facets and six side facets. Signed with a "P1993" cane in the base. Edition size: 300/156 made.

1993E

FUCHSIA
A pink and amethyst fuchsia with leaves and three buds on a white lace ground. Signed with a "P1993" cane in the base. Edition size: 300/300 made.

BLACK OVERLAY
A multicolored bouquet on a clear ground, enclosed within a black single overlay. One top facet, twelve side facets, and a star-cut base. Signed with a "P" cane at the base of the stem. This appears to be the first black overlay made by any maker. Edition size: 300/199 made.

1993F

THREE-DIMENSIONAL BOUQUET
A three-dimensional bouquet of four flowers and three buds above a blue flash. One top facet, twenty-four side facets, and a star-cut base. Signed with a "P" cane at the base of the bouquet. Edition size: 250/250 made.

1993G

MAGNUM CONCENTRIC MILLEFIORI
A magnum weight containing a variety of complex square and bull's-eye canes arranged in a concentric pattern with a twelve-petaled blue flower in the center. Usually faceted with one top facet and eight side facets. A few are not faceted. Signed with a "P1993" cane in the base and also signed with a "PM^{C}D" cane (for the maker, Peter McDougall) in the next to the outside ring. Edition size: 50/40 made.

1993

MINIATURE PANSY
An amethyst and yellow pansy with two buds on a white lace ground. One top facet and eight side facets. Signed with a "P1994" cane in the base. Edition size: 400/280 made.

1994A

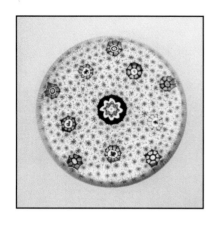

1994B

CARPET GROUND
Five picture canes and five complex canes spaced around a large complex center cane, all on a carpet ground of identical canes, each of which has an orange center surrounded by yellow and then white. Signed with a "P1994" cane in the base. Edition size: 300/150 made.

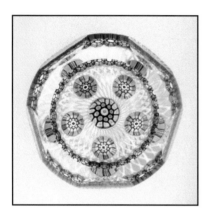

1994C

MILLEFIORI BASKET
A complex center cane surrounded by five complex canes and a garland of alternating amethyst and blue canes on a white double spiral latticinio ground. Complex cane colors vary. One top facet and five side facets. Signed with a "P1994" cane in the base. Edition size: 300/145 made.

1994D

THISTLE
Five Scottish thistles surrounding a complex center cane and encircled by a looping garland of white stardust canes, all on a black or translucent blue ground. One top facet and five side facets. Signed with a "P1994" cane in the base. Edition size: 300/220 made.

1994E

BOUQUET ON CUSHION
A multicolored bouquet containing a large central pink flower on a webbed royal blue cushion ground. Signed with a "P1994" cane in the base. Edition size: 300/187 made.

FRUIT

Two oranges, two bunches of grapes, a pear, a lemon and several cherries on a bed of leaves on a clear ground. One top facet, eighteen side facets, and a feather-cut base. Scratch-signed "P" near the feather cutting. Edition size: 300/266 made.

1994F

OVERLAY BOUQUET

A bouquet of two flowers, four buds, and three leaves on a clear ground within a translucent gold-ruby overlay. One large top facet, geometric faceting around the sides, and a grid-cut base. Scratch-signed "P" on the overlay near the base. Edition size: 300/214 made.

1994G

MAGNUM BOUQUET

An intricate three-dimensional bouquet of flowers and buds tied with an amethyst striped bow on a clear ground. One top facet, twenty-four side facets, and a grid-cut base. Scratch-signed "P" next to the base. Edition size: 35/29 made.

1994

COMPLEX MILLEFIORI

A complex millefiori design with six segments separated by radial twists and featuring a ring of blue and white half-canes on a translucent ruby ground. Cane colors vary. One top facet and six side facets. Signed with a "P1995" cane in the base. Edition size: 300/191 made.

1995A

1995B

FLOWERS ON LACE
A lampwork flower surrounded by three lamp-work flowers alternating with three picture canes on a white lace ground. Flower colors are pink or blue. Signed with a "P1995" cane in the base. Edition size: 300/204 made.

1995C

CROWN
A crown of red, white, and blue twists enclosed within a crown of spaced white latticinio rods and topped by a blue lampwork flower with two blue buds and leaves. Signed with a "P1995" cane in the base. Perthshire's first crown within a crown. Edition size: 350/284 made.

1995D

DAISIES
A central white daisy and bud surrounded by a ring of spaced canes and a garland of daisy-shaped canes on a translucent dark amethyst-blue ground. One top facet and six side facets. Signed with a "P1995" cane in the base. Edition size: 300/140 made.

1995E

ROSE BOUQUET
A bouquet of one pale lemon rose, one ruby rose, three buds, and four green leaves on a clear ground. One top facet, twenty-four side facets, and a star-cut base. Scratch-signed "P" next to the base. Edition size: 300/251 made.

DOUBLE OVERLAY BUTTERFLIES
Two intricate butterflies hovering over a bouquet of two pink flowers and green leaves within a double overlay of amethyst-red over white. One top facet, six large and six small side facets, and a star-cut base. Scratch-signed "P" next to the base. Edition size: 300/228 made.

1995F

FLASH OVERLAY
A bouquet of two Pinguicula Grandiflora-style flowers, three rose buds, and two lupines, tied together with a yellow bow, all within a highly cut blue flash overlay. One top facet with six side facets and fancy cuts all over the sides. Scratch-signed "P" on the base. Edition size: 250/143 made.

1995G

MAGNUM MILLEFIORI
A six-segment patterned millefiori design featuring six colored picture canes surrounding a central horse and jockey cane, all on a ruby ground. Most have one top facet and six side facets. A few are domed. Signed with a "P1995" cane in the base. Edition size: 50/35 made.

1995

MINIATURE FLOWER
A ruby lampwork flower and bud within a garland of millefiori canes on a clear ground. Garland color is blue or green. One top facet, six side facets, and a star-cut base. Scratch-signed "P" on the basal rim. Edition size: 400.

1996A

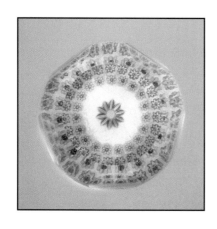

1996B

FLOWER ON LACE
A blue flower on a lace ground surrounded by two rings of daisy canes. One top facet and five side facets. Signed with a "P1996" cane in the base. Edition size: 250.

1996C

CROWN
Red and blue twists alternating with white latticinio rods placed over a ruby layer to form a crown. Visible through the single top facet is a white flower with three buds and leaves. Signed with a "P1996" cane in the base. Edition size: 300.

1996D

PINK FLOWER
A large pink flower with yellow and orange stamens and two pink buds on a stem with large leaves on a translucent blue ground. One top facet and twelve side facets. Unsigned, but the edition number is scratched on the base. Edition size: 250.

1996E

LADYBIRD
Three light blue flowers with yellow stamens, stems, and green leaves, on a clear ground. On a leaf to the left rests a red and black ladybird. One top facet and twelve side facets. Signed with a "P" cane next to the stem. Edition size: 250.

DOUBLE OVERLAY
A bouquet of five flowers and three buds on a green cushion ground within a double overlay of green over white. One top facet and twelve side facets. Signed with a "P1996" cane in the base. Edition size: 200.

1996F

BLOSSOM
Seven pink flowers and eight buds on branches with many leaves on a clear ground. One top facet, sixteen side facets, and a star-cut base. Signed with a "P" cane at the base of the branch. Edition size: 200.

1996G

MAGNUM BOUQUET
Eight blue buds on a curving branch with striped leaves and roots on a clear ground. One top facet, forty side facets, and a feather-cut base. Scratch-signed "P" near the edge of the base. Edition size: 25.

1996

MINIATURE FLOWER
A miniature weight containing a pink or blue flower surrounded by a matching cane garland. The weight is overlaid with thin colored rods in pink or blue to match the flowers. One top facet. Scratch-signed "P" on the base. Edition size: 350.

1997A

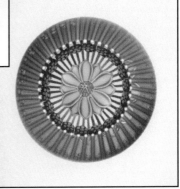

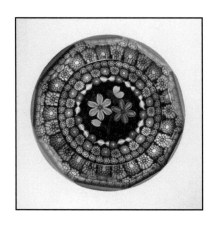

1997B

MILLEFIORI AND FLOWERS
A bouquet of two flowers and three buds surrounded by a ring of nine complex canes alternating with nine twists and then two more rings of canes, all on a translucent amethyst ground. One top facet and nine side facets. Signed with a "P1997" cane in the base. Edition size: 250.

1997C

GARLAND
A central six-lobed garland of stardust canes surrounded by six blue florets, each with two lampwork leaves, all enclosed by a looping garland of white stardust canes on a translucent gold-ruby cushion ground. One top facet and twelve side facets. Signed with a "P1997" cane in the base. Edition size: 250.

1997D

BLUE BOUQUET
Six blue flowers with yellow stamens on a bed of green leaves on a clear ground. One top facet, twenty-four side facets, and a diamond-cut base. Signed with a "P" cane next to the base of the bouquet. Edition size: 300.

1997E

FLASH OVERLAY
Bouquet of four flowers, three buds and several leaves on a clear ground, all within a blue flash overlay. One top facet with thirty oval side facets and thirty notch side facets. Star-cut base. Scratch-signed "P" on the overlay near the base. Edition size: 250.

THREE-DIMENSIONAL BOUQUET
Four flowers and three buds on a bed of leaves over a latticinio cushion ground. One top facet with twenty-four side facets. Scratch-signed "P" on the base. Edition size: 200.

1997F

SNAKE
A brown rattlesnake with yellow and black spots coiled in a desert setting with a cactus and a wild flower. Scratch-signed "P" on the base. Edition size: 150.

1997G

MAGNUM MUSHROOM
A large mushroom of a closepacked design with yellow and blue strips down the stem. Many facets are placed all over the weight. Scratch-signed "P" on the base. Some signed "PMᶜD" (for the maker, Peter McDougall) in the base. Edition size: 25.

1997

Christmas
Weights

CHRISTMAS HOLLY
Three holly leaves and four red berries on a
white lace ground. Signed "P1971" in canes in
the base. Edition size: 250/250 made.

1971

CHRISTMAS MISTLETOE
A sprig of mistletoe with berries surrounded by
a ring of green and white canes alternating with
red and white canes on an opaque red ground.
Signed "P1972" in canes in the base. Edition
size: 300/300 made.

1972

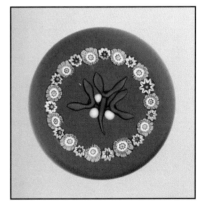

CHRISTMAS ROBIN
Crown of green and white twists with a colored
picture cane of a robin at the center. Signed
with a "P1974" cane in the base. Edition size:
325/317 made.

1974

1975

CHRISTMAS FLOWER
A white rose with small green leaves and a bud on a clear ground. One top facet and a star-cut base. Signed "P" in the center of the flower. Edition size: 350/347 made.

1976

CHRISTMAS POINSETTIA
A red poinsettia with green leaves surrounded by a ring of green canes alternating with white canes on a clear ground. Signed with a "P" cane on the underside of the poinsettia. Edition size: 350/316 made.

1977

CHRISTMAS BELLS
Tiny pink canes and white stardust canes closepacked in the shape of two bells which are looped together by a string of green canes on a translucent ruby ground. One top facet and eight side facets. Signed with a "P1977" cane in the base. Edition size: 325/318 made.

1978

CHRISTMAS HOLLY
Three holly leaves with red berries in the center of a circle of green millefiori canes on an opaque white ground with a white overlay. One top facet and sixteen side facets. Signed with a "P1978" cane in the base. This is the only white single overlay ever made by Perthshire. Edition size: 325/322 made.

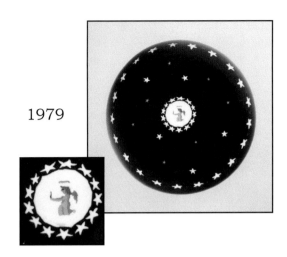

1979

CHRISTMAS ANGEL
A colored picture cane of an angel with a border of millefiori stars surrounded by randomly placed white stars and an outer ring of spaced stars on a dark blue ground. Domed or with one top facet and five side facets. Signed with a "P1979" cane in the base. Edition size: 325/307 made.

CHRISTMAS CANDLE
A red candle with holly leaves and berries on white lace over a red, blue, or green ground. Domed or with one top facet and five side facets. Signed with a "P1980" cane in the base. Edition size: 300/295 made.

1980

CHRISTMAS SILHOUETTES
Five colored picture canes with Christmas themes, spaced around a complex center "doily" cane and encircled by a border of canes similar to the "doily," all on a translucent green ground. Signed with a "P1981" cane in the base. Edition size: 300/225 made.

1981

CHRISTMAS SHEPHERD
A shepherd with a lamb against a starry night sky, all surrounded by a garland of green millefiori canes on an opaque black ground. The shepherd's cloak is either green or brown. One top facet. Signed with a "P1982" cane in the base. Edition size: 350/318 made.

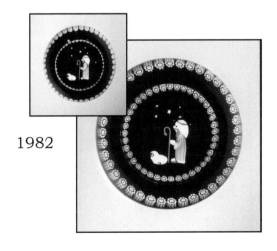

1982

1983

CHRISTMAS HOLLY WREATH
A holly wreath made from individual leaf clusters and berries tied with a red and green bow on a white lace ground. Signed with a "P1983" cane in the base. Edition size: 350/343 made.

1984

CHRISTMAS BOUQUET
A white rose, a red poinsettia, and holly leaves with berries in a bouquet on a clear ground. Domed or with one top facet and six side facets. Diamond-cut base. Signed with a "P" cane at the base of the stems. Edition size: 350/298 made.

1985

CHRISTMAS CROWN
A crown made with white latticinio alternating with red and green twists with a large colored picture cane of a decorated candle at the top. Signed with a "P1985" cane in the base. Edition size: 300/300 made.

1986

CHRISTMAS CANDLE
A large red candle with holly leaves and red berries at its base floating above a basket of green staves alternating with red and white latticinio staves. Signed "P" in one of the green staves of the basket. Edition size: 350/338 made.

CHRISTMAS ROSE

A central white rose, two sprigs of holly with berries, white stars, and "Noel" written in script on a deep blue ground. One top facet and six side facets. Signed with a "P1987" cane in the base. Edition size: 400/332 made.

1987

THREE KINGS

Three robed figures, representing the Three Kings following the Star of Bethlehem, shown on an opaque dark ground. One top facet and six side facets. Signed with a "P1988" cane in the base. Edition size: 350/307 made.

1988

CHRISTMAS BOUQUET

A bouquet of two poinsettias and holly leaves with berries on an opaque white ground. One top facet and six side facets. Signed with a "P1989" cane in the base. Edition size: 350/340 made.

1989

PARTRIDGE IN A PEAR TREE

A partridge in a pear tree in a large colored picture cane surrounded by four sprigs of holly leaves and four colored picture canes of a robin and then by two rings of millefiori canes, all on a translucent dark blue ground. Domed or with a top facet and six side facets. Signed with a "P1990" cane in the base. Edition size: 400/341 made.

1990

71

1991

CHRISTMAS TURTLE DOVE
A white turtle dove with outspread wings of white stardust canes, carrying an olive branch on a translucent dark blue ground. The entire design is surrounded by a ring of white stars. One top facet and six side facets. Signed with a "P1991" cane in the base. The canes making up the dove contain more than 4000 stars. Edition size: 375/288 made.

1992

CHRISTMAS SNOWMAN
A snowman with a broom, standing under a starry sky, surrounded by a ring of alternating red and green canes on a black ground. One top facet. Signed with a "P1992" cane in the base. Edition size: 250/224 made.

1993

NATIVITY SCENE
A large central colored picture cane featuring a Nativity scene with Mary and Child set in a five-pointed star of yellow stardust canes outlined by white latticinio rods, all on a translucent blue ground. The area between the star points is filled by blue canes and a white star cane and bordered by red and green canes. One top facet and five side facets. Signed with a "P1993" cane in the base. Edition size: 250/250 made.

1994

CHRISTMAS BELLS
Two bells, composed of white stardust canes and tied together with an amber millefiori bow, with two holly leaves below, all surrounded by a ring of alternating red and blue millefiori canes on a translucent green ground. One top facet. Signed with a "P1994" cane in the base. Edition size: 200/200 made.

CHRISTMAS ROBIN

A central colored picture cane of a robin with several stars above and a sprig of mistletoe below, all surrounded first by a ring of red canes alternating with short latticinio rods and then by a ring of blue and white canes alternating with white canes, all on a translucent red ground. One top facet and six side facets. Signed with a "P1995" cane in the base. Edition size: 250/250 made.

1995

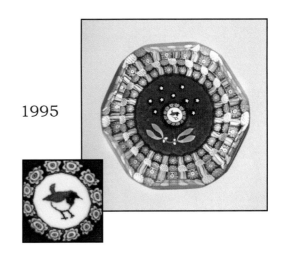

CHRISTMAS BOUQUET

A bouquet of mistletoe, holly leaves, and a poinsettia flower surrounded by a ring of green canes on an opaque white ground. One top facet and five side facets. Signed with a "P1996" cane in the base. Edition size: 250.

1996

Limited Edition and General Range Weights

In the descriptions of the Limited Edition and General Range Weights, the following standards are used. The Glossary contains additional definitions of the terms used.

SIZES: All sizes are approximate.
    Magnum: Diameter of more than 3 inches. Specific sizes are given.
    Large: Diameter of approximately 3 inches
    Medium: Diameter of approximately 2-1/2 inches
    Small: Diameter of approximately 2 inches
    Miniature: Diameter of less than 2 inches
    Bottles: Heights include the stopper. Diameters are given at the widest point.

COLOR VARIATIONS: Ground and cane colors vary unless a specific color is indicated. Different cane colors can cause major differences in the appearance of the weight by accenting different parts of the design.

BASES: All paperweight bases are hollow-ground unless otherwise indicated. The bases of bottles and glasses vary and are not specified.

PATTERNS: Designs are described from the center out. The number of millefiori rings and radial twists, as well as the number of canes in groups, may occasionally vary. See the next page for an enlarged photograph showing how millefiori patterns are described in this book.

Some weights were issued in both domed and faceted versions of the same design. This is indicated in the individual descriptions; however, only one version (either domed or faceted) is shown in the photographs. When a photograph of a faceted version is shown, it is designated by the letter "A," per the factory literature. It should be noted that Perthshire also designated some design or size changes by the letter A (PP19A, PP133A, PP156A, PP178A, for example). These are treated as separate model numbers and are listed separately in the text.

SIGNATURES/DATES: The standard signature of the letter "P" in a cane is referred to as a "P" cane and is undated unless stated otherwise. When the term, dated "P" cane, is used, it refers to a cane containing both the letter "P" and a date showing the year in which the weight was issued. Photographs of various signature/date canes are shown in the Identification Chapter.

EDITION SIZES: Edition sizes are unlimited unless stated otherwise. Limited Edition sizes vary from 250 to 400 per year.

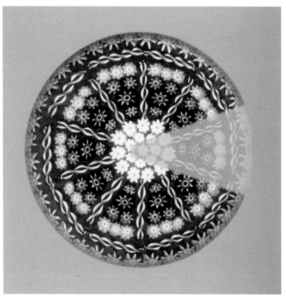

PP1

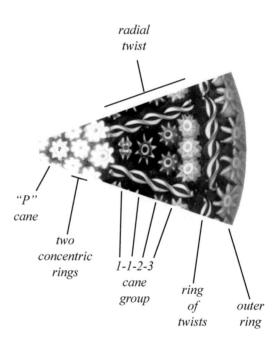

Section of a PP1 showing how the cane groups are counted. This pattern has a center "P" cane, two concentric rings of canes, and ten radial twists separating cane groups of 1-1-2-3, then a ring of twists and an outer ring of canes.

Pre - 1978

Pre - 1978

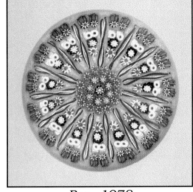

Pre - 1978

PP1

Large millefiori weight with an opaque or translucent color ground. The PP1 comes in three distinct designs. Most weights made before 1982 have a central cane surrounded by two concentric rings and thirteen or fourteen radial twists separating cane groups of 1-1-2-2. Some very early PP1s have considerably fewer radial twists and weights with a larger number of radials also exist. Weights made before 1978 are unsigned and have a fire-polished base. Weights made from 1978 through 1981 have a center "P" cane and a hollow-ground base. This pattern was also identified as PP6 from 1972 through 1977 (when PP1 weights were not signed). In weights made from 1982 through 1997, the pattern has a center "P" cane, two concentric rings of canes, and ten radial twists separating cane groups of 1-1-2-3, then a ring of twists and an outer ring of canes. The PP58 also has this design, but it as a top facet. Made 1969 - 1997.

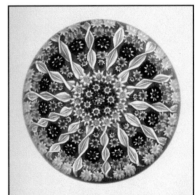

1978 - 1981

1982 - 1997

Pre - 1978

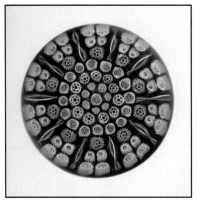

Pre - 1978

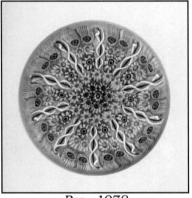

Pre - 1978

PP2

Medium millefiori weight with a color ground and a pattern similar to the first PP1 design. Weights made before 1978 are unsigned and have a fire-polished base. Weights made since 1978 have a center "P" cane and a hollow-ground base. The PP59 also has this design, but it has a top facet. Made 1969 - 1997.

Pre - 1978

1978 - 1997

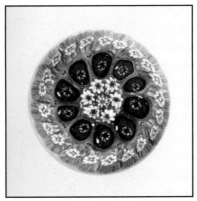

1969 - 1973

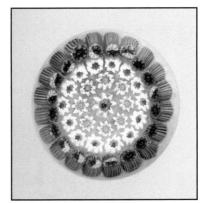

1969 - 1973

1969 - 1973

PP3

Miniature concentric millefiori weight with a color ground. The center cane is usually surrounded by four rings of canes. Weights made from 1969 through 1973 have a fire-polished base and are not signed. Weights made since 1984 have a hollow-ground base and are signed with a center "P" cane. Made 1969 - 1973 and 1984 - 1997. A few weights were made in 1983, but not exported.

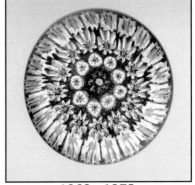

1984 - 1997

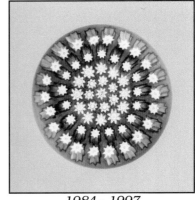

1984 - 1997

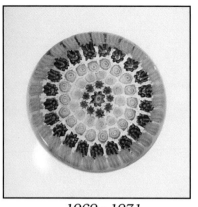

1969 - 1971

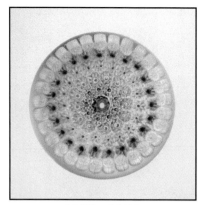

1969 - 1971

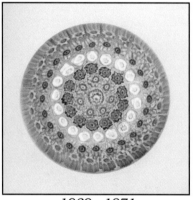

1969 - 1971

PP4

Medium concentric millefiori weight. It may be signed with a "P" cane in the outer ring. Weights made in 1969 through 1971 have a flat, polished, star-cut base and weights made since 1972 have a hollow-ground base. From 1969 through 1992, all weights were made with a clear ground. Weights made in 1993 and 1994 have a color ground. Made 1969 - 1994.

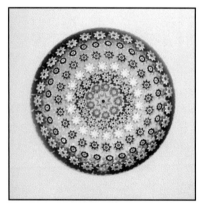

1972 - 1992

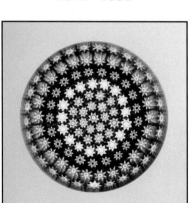

1993 - 1994

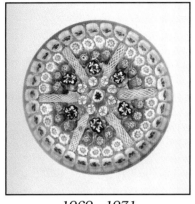

1969 - 1971

1969 - 1971

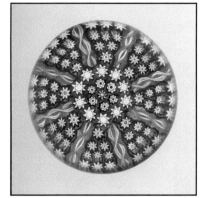

1972 - 1995

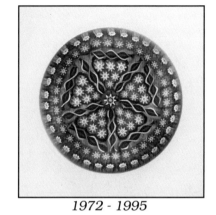

PP5

1972 - 1995

Medium millefiori weight with a translucent color ground. The designs and patterns vary, but all include a combination of simple canes and twists. Some are signed with a "P" cane in the setup. Weights made in 1969 through 1971 have a flat, polished, star-cut base and weights made since 1972 have a hollow-ground base. From 1969 through 1995, weights were not faceted. Weights made in 1996 and thereafter have a top facet and six side facets. The PP5 and PP60 designs are the same, but the PP60 has a single top facet. Made 1969 - 1997.

1972 - 1995

1996 - 1997

1972 - 1995

1969 - 1971   PP6

1972 - 1977

From 1969 - 1971, the PP5 and PP6 were identical in size (medium) and had star-cut bases. The only difference was in color. The PP5 had an amber ground; the PP6, a green ground. Weights made in 1972 through 1977 are large with a pattern identical to that of the first PP1 (cane groups of 1-1-2-2). The only difference is that when the PP1 was unsigned and had a fire-polished base, the PP6 had a center "P" cane and a hollow-ground base. The PP6 was discontinued after 1977 when the PP1 became signed with a center "P" cane. Made 1969 -1977.

PP7

Medium two-layered "fountain" weight with a translucent color ground. Layers of canes and cane chips are drawn down at the corners and the center to form a two-layered "fountain" with bubbles placed at the depressions. The base is fire-polished. This weight was named "Aladdin's Cave" in early Perthshire literature and was described as having a lower layer "reflecting" the upper layer. Unsigned. Not made for export. Made 1969 - 1971.

PP8

Large three-layered "fountain" weight with a translucent color ground. Layers of canes and cane chips are drawn down at the corners and the center to form a three-layered "fountain" with bubbles placed at the depressions. The base is fire-polished. This weight was named "Aladdin's Cave" in early Perthshire literature and was described as having lower layers "reflecting" the upper layers. Unsigned. Not made for export. Made 1969 - 1971.

Large clear weight containing a six-petaled tulip with a single center stamen. It was made in assorted colors and has a flat, polished base. Unsigned. Made 1969 - 1971.

PP9

Medium millefiori weight with five cane clusters surrounding a central cluster on a translucent color ground. Each cluster contains six or seven canes in a ring around a central cane. The weight has a flat, polished, star-cut base and is unsigned. Made 1969 - 1973.

PP10

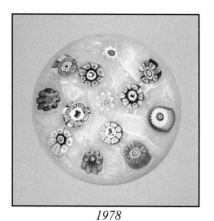

1978

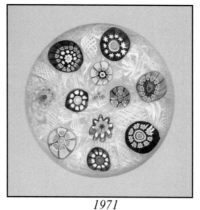

1971

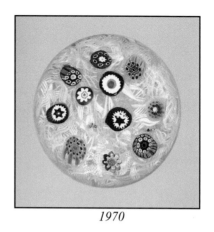

1970

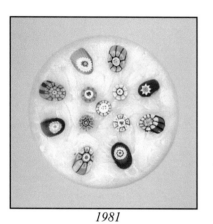

1981

PP11

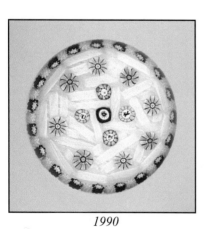

1983

Large spaced millefiori weight with a white lace ground or a ground of white latticinio twists laid out in various "checker" patterns. Weights made in 1972 and thereafter contain one or more silhouette or picture canes. Weights made in 1983 through 1990 have an outer ring of canes. Weights made in 1991 and 1992 have a center cane with a ring of six spaced silhouette or colored picture canes and an outer ring of seven spaced complex canes on a structured pattern of latticinio rods. Weights made through 1974 have a flat, polished base and weights made after that have a hollow-ground base. The letter "P" and the date are in a cane or canes in the setup in weights made through 1989. Weights made in 1990 have a "PP1990" cane in the setup. Weights made in 1991 and 1992 are signed with a dated "P" cane in the base. Made 1969 - 1992. Limited edition.

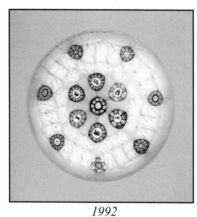

1990

1992

Blue (1969)

Green (1970)

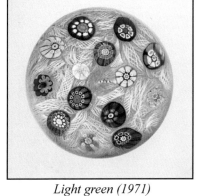

Light green (1971)

Large spaced millefiori weight similar to PP11. It was made with two distinct types of ground. Weights made from 1969 through 1975 have a base of translucent color under the white lace, and weights made after 1975 have a colored lace ground. Colors are: 1969--blue, 1970--green, 1971--light green, 1972--blue, 1973--blue, 1974--blue, 1975--indigo, 1976--blue, and 1977--blue. Weights made before 1975 have a flat, polished base and later weights have a hollow-ground base. The letter "P" and the date are in the setup. Made 1969 - 1977. Limited edition.

PP12

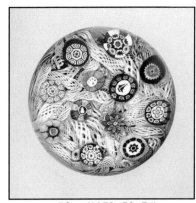

Blue (1972, 73, 74)

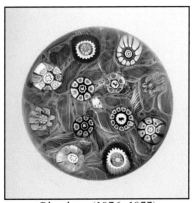

Blue lace (1976, 1977)

Indigo (1975)

85

Amethyst (1971, 72, 73)

Blue (1970)

Honey amber (1975)

PP13

Pink lace (1976)

Large spaced millefiori weight similar to PP12, except for different colors by year, as follows: 1970--blue, 1971--amethyst, 1972--amethyst, 1973--amethyst, 1975--honey amber, 1976--pink, 1977--orange. As with the PP12, weights made in 1970 through 1975 have a base of translucent color and weights made after 1975 have a colored lace ground. Weights made before 1975 have a flat, polished base and later weights have a hollow-ground base. The letter "P" and the date are in the setup. Made 1970 - 1973 and 1975 - 1977. Limited edition.

Orange lace (1977)

Medium millefiori weight containing five cane clusters surrounding a larger center cane cluster on a clear ground. It has a large top facet, five side facets, and a flat, polished, star-cut base. The center cluster contains a letter designating the year of manufacture, e.g., "A" for 1969, "B" for 1970, "Z" for 1994. The weight has no other signature. This is the only weight made with each letter of the alphabet. Made 1969 - 1994. Limited edition.

PP14

"A" for 1969   *"Z" for 1994*

Large faceted millefiori inkwell with matching stopper (6 in. high, 3-1/2 in. dia.). The bottom of the bottle and the stopper contain a close-packed millefiori pattern on a translucent blue ground. The bottle has two rows of facets, with each row containing four large and four small oval facets. The stopper has a single top facet and two rows of four oval facets each. Signed with a "P" cane in the stopper setup. Made 1969 - 1994.

PP15

Millefiori doorknob with assorted backgrounds and patterns on a metal base. The pattern is not specific as a means of identification, but is often similar to the PP2 design. Made 1969 - 1970.

PP16

PP17

Millefiori doorknob with assorted backgrounds and patterns on a brass base. The pattern is not specific as a means of identification, but is often similar to a PP2 design. Made 1969 - 1973.

PP18

Millefiori doorknob on a brass base. It has a closepacked or close concentric design on a blue ground. May be signed with a "P" cane in the setup. Made 1969 - 1978 and 1984 - 1997.

PP18A

Millefiori doorknob on a brass base. The pattern has five cane clusters surrounding a larger cane cluster. The setup is usually on a blue ground, but a few were made with a red, green, or black ground. Signed with a "P" cane in the center. Made 1995 - 1997.

1970

1987

Large scrambled (end-of-day) millefiori weight. Weights made prior to 1992 are slightly smaller (2-3/4 in.) and have a clear ground. They are signed with the letter "P" and a date in a cane or canes in the setup. Weights made in 1992 and thereafter have a black ground and are signed with a dated "P" cane in the base. Made 1969 - 1980 and 1987 - 1997. Limited edition.

PP19

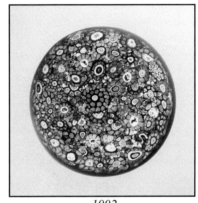

1992

Small scrambled (end-of-day) millefiori weight with a black ground. Signed with a dated "P" cane in the base. Made 1995 - 1997. Limited edition.

PP19A

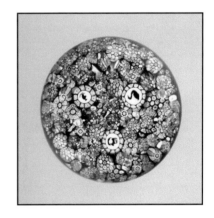

Medium swirl weight with a complex center cane and multicolored spiral threads extending outward and wrapped around to the bottom. The weight has a clear ground and a flat, polished base. Unsigned. Made 1971 - 1975.

PP20

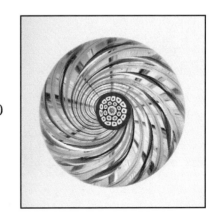

PP21

Large swirl weight with a complex center cane and multicolored spiral threads extending outward and wrapped around to the bottom. It has a clear ground. The base may be hollow-ground, fire-polished, or flat. Unsigned. Perthshire catalogues show this weight from 1974 through 1977. Perthshirc literature from 1971 shows PP21 as a "seaweed weight on seabed effect." However, factory production records do not support this. There is no mention of a PP21 of any type in 1972. A 1971 dealer's literature shows a photo of a seaweed weight and designates it "P9." This is not a Perthshire number.

PP22

Small scent bottle with stopper (5-1/2 in. high, 2-1/2 in. dia.). The bottom of the bottle has a concentric millefiori pattern on a translucent color ground. The stopper has strands of color matching the ground. In bottles made from 1973 through 1982, the bottom contains a center cane and four concentric rings. In those made after 1982, the bottom contains a center "P" cane and five concentric rings. The body is widest at the base. Made 1973 - 1996.

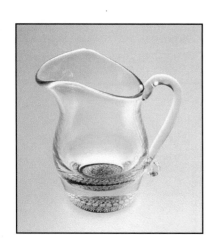

PP23

Cream jug or pitcher with a concentric millefiori pattern on a translucent color ground in the bottom. The pitcher is approximately 4-1/4 inches high and has a diameter of 2-3/4 inches. The base is hollow-ground. Unsigned. Made 1973 - 1975.

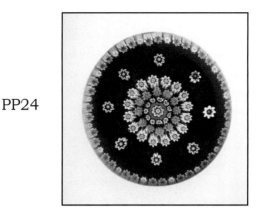

PP24

Large concentric millefiori weight with four close concentric rings of canes, a spaced concentric ring, and then an outer close concentric ring, all on a translucent color ground. Signed with a "P" and the date in canes in the base. Made 1972 - 1973. Limited edition.

PP25

Medium millefiori weight with a center cane surrounded by one ring of canes, six short radial twists separating cane groups of 1-2-3-4, and then two outer rings of canes on a translucent color ground. Signed with a "P" cane in the setup. Made 1974 - 1975. Limited edition.

PP26

Large millefiori weight with a center cane surrounded by one ring of canes, then seven or eight short radial twists separating cane groups of 1-2-3, and then three outer rings of canes on a translucent color ground. Signed with a "P" cane in the setup. Made 1974. Limited edition.

PP27

Large millefiori weight with a center colored picture cane of a thistle surrounded by two rings of canes and then nine pairs of radial twists separating cane groups of 1-2, all on a white lace ground. Signed with a dated "P" cane in the base. Made 1974 - 1975. Limited edition.

PP28

Large millefiori weight. Weights made before 1978 have a center cane surrounded by two rings of canes, then eight or nine short radial twists separating cane groups of 1-2-3 or 1-1-2-3, and then two outer rings of canes. They are not faceted. Weights made from 1978 through 1982 have only one ring surrounding the center cane and nine radial twists and have a single top facet. All have a clear ground and are signed with a "P" cane in the outer ring. Made 1975 - 1982.

PP29

Sugar bowl with a bottom that contains concentric rings of millefiori canes on a translucent color ground. The bowl is approximately 2-1/4 inches high and 3-1/2 inches in diameter and has a hollow-ground base. Unsigned. Made 1975 only.

PP30

Large millefiori weight with a star-shaped pattern outlined by twist canes on a translucent color ground. Two different star-shaped patterns have been identified as PP30. Both patterns are filled with millefiori canes and have cane groups of 1-3-4-5-6 between the points. Signed with a dated "P" cane in the base. Made 1976 - 1979. Limited edition.

PP31

Large millefiori weight with a center complex cane surrounded by one ring of canes, then eight to ten short radial twists separating cane groups of 1-2, a ring of canes, a ring of twists, and an outer ring of canes, all on a translucent color ground. Signed with a dated "P" cane in the base. Made 1976 - 1978. Limited edition.

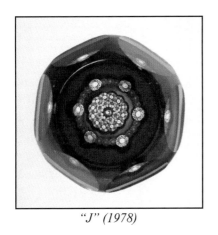

"J" (1978)

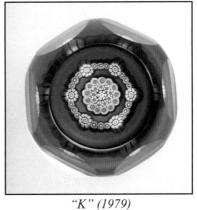

"K" (1979)

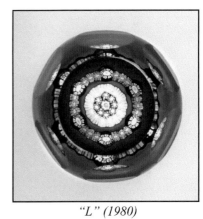

"L" (1980)

Small or miniature millefiori weight with a translucent color ground and various patterns and faceting. The center cane contains a letter representing the year, beginning with "J" for 1978 and continuing through "R" for 1986. Limited edition.

PP32

"M" (1981)

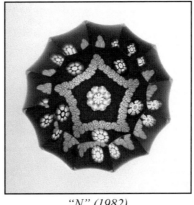

"N" (1982)

"O" (1983)

"P" (1984)

"Q" (1985)

"R" (1986)

PP33

Large millefiori weight with an overall pattern of a Maltese cross filled with cane groups of 4-4-4-4-4 on a translucent color ground. The triangles between the arms of the cross are outlined by twists and filled with small canes, all of the same color. The weight has a large top facet and is signed with a dated "P" cane in the base. Perthshire referred to this weight as "A Formal Garden." Made 1978 - 1979. Limited edition.

PP34

Large millefiori weight with four radials extending from a center cane, resulting in a cross. Each radial consists of a row of canes with a twist on each side. The radials separate cane groups of 1-2-3-4-5-7. The weight has a translucent color ground. Signed with a dated "P" cane in the base. Made 1978 - 1979. Limited edition.

PP35

Large millefiori "chessboard" weight with twist canes outlining five squares laid out in a cross pattern on a translucent color ground. Each square contains one large cane surrounded by a square of smaller canes. The center square contains eight small canes and the surrounding squares each contain twelve small canes. Four triangular cane groups of 1-2-3-4-5 complete the pattern. Signed with a dated "P" cane in the base. Made 1979 - 1980. Limited edition.

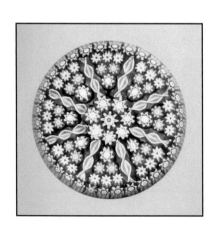

PP36

Large millefiori weight the same as PP5, except for size. The designs and patterns vary, but all include a combination of canes and twists on a translucent color ground. Signed with a "P" cane in the setup. Made 1979 only.

Large concentric millefiori weight with a center cane surrounded by five rings of large canes on a color ground. Signed with a "P1979" cane in the base. Limited edition.

PP37

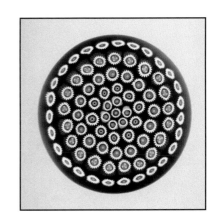

Medium concentric millefiori weight with a large complex center cane surrounded by a ring of medium canes, a ring of spaced large canes, a ring of twists, and an outer close ring of canes, all on a translucent color ground. Signed with a "P1980" cane in the base. Limited edition.

PP38

Medium concentric millefiori weight with a complex center cane surrounded by a ring of small canes, a hexagon of canes with a large cane at each point, a hexagon of twists, and two outer rings of canes, all on a translucent color ground. Signed with a "P1980" cane in the base. Limited edition.

PP39

Large millefiori weight with a pattern of two pentagons. The center cane is surrounded by a pentagon filled with small millefiori canes and outlined with twists. A larger pentagon, also filled with millefiori canes and outlined with twists, surrounds the inner pentagon and is angularly offset from it. The weight has a translucent color ground. Signed with a "P1980" cane in the base. Limited edition.

PP40

PP41

Large millefiori weight with a complex center cane surrounded by a ring of close canes, a ring of spaced canes, and then six radials, each consisting of a single row of canes with a twist on each side. The radials separate triangular cane groups of 1-2-3-4 or 1-2-3-4-5 and outer twists complete the triangles. The weight has a translucent color ground. Signed with a "P1980" cane in the base. Limited edition.

1992 - 1994

PP42

Small scent bottle (5-1/2 in. high, 2-1/2 in. dia.). Bottles made from 1980 through 1989 are spherical and the bottom contains a concentric millefiori pattern with five rings of canes surrounding a center "P" cane. Bottles made in 1990 and 1991 are similar, but are pear-shaped. The tall, tapered stopper contains twisted colored threads in all bottles made before 1992. Bottles made from 1992 through 1994 are teardrop shaped (7-1/2 in. high, 2-3/4 in. dia.) with a clear foot and are unsigned. They contain an upright pink rose. The tear-drop-shaped stopper contains five straight pink threads. Made 1980 - 1994.

1990 - 1991

1980 - 1989

1980 - 1983

1987 - 1994

Shot glass made in two distinct patterns (1-7/8 in. dia., 2-3/4 in. high). In glasses made from 1980 through 1983, the bottom contains a single red lampwork flower with a "P" cane in the center on a translucent blue ground. The lower half of the outside of the glass is fluted. In glasses made from 1987 through 1994, the bottom has a concentric millefiori pattern of four rings of canes around a central "P" cane on a translucent blue ground. The outside is not fluted. Made 1980 - 1983 and 1987 - 1994.

PP43

Medium millefiori weight with a star pattern made of twist canes. Within the star, a complex center cane is surrounded by two rings of canes. A single large cane is located within each of the star points and five others are placed around the outside of the star. The points of the star divide an outer ring of canes into five segments of five canes each. The weight has a translucent color ground. Signed with a "P1981" cane in the base. Limited edition.

PP44

Large millefiori weight with six pairs of short twist canes outlining six spokes around a central concentric pattern of canes and twists. The central pattern consists of a large complex center cane, a ring of millefiori canes, a ring of twists, and another ring of canes. Each spoke contains four rows of three canes each. Triangular cane groups between the spokes are in a 1-2-3-4 pattern. The weight has a translucent color ground. Signed with a "P1981" cane in the base. Limited edition.

PP45

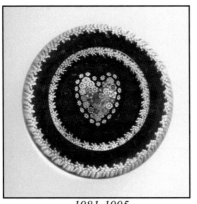

1981-1995

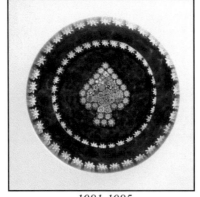

1981-1985

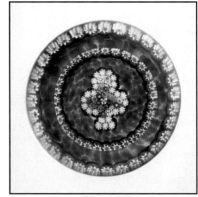

1981-1985

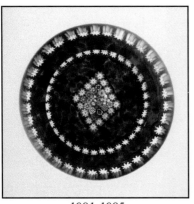

1981-1985

PP46

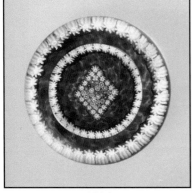

1986

Medium weight originally made in four separate millefiori patterns surrounded by a ring of canes on a translucent color ground. The designs are: a heart on a ruby ground; a diamond on an amethyst ground; a club on a green ground; and a spade on a blue ground. In each case, the center design has an outer edge row of canes, all of the same color, and is filled with closepacked canes. From 1981 through 1985, all four patterns were made. In 1986, heart and diamond weights were made with a ruby ground and, thereafter, only the heart was produced. In weights made in 1996, the heart is filled with closepacked canes, all of the same color, and there are two perimeter rows, each of a single color. Weights made in 1997 have the original heart design of a multicolored closepack with one perimeter row. All weights have a single top facet, except for the heart made in 1997, which has a top facet and five or six side facets. All weights are signed with a "P" cane in the base. Made 1981 - 1997.

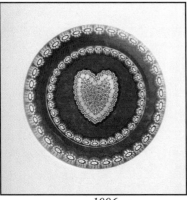

1996

1997

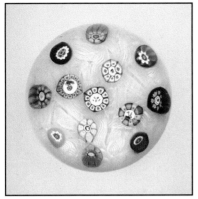

White (1981, 1982)

Green (1983)

Blue (1984)

Small millefiori weight made in several distinct patterns, each on a lace ground. Weights made from 1981 through 1989 have a central dated "P" cane surrounded by four spaced silhouette or colored picture canes and an outer ring of eight spaced complex millefiori canes. The lace colors are: 1981--white; 1982--white; 1983--green; 1984--blue; 1985--amethyst; 1986--black; 1987--orange; 1988--blue; and 1989--ruby. Weights made from 1990 through 1992 have a central silhouette or colored picture cane surrounded by four spaced silhouette or colored picture canes and an outer ring of close millefiori canes on white lace. The canes in the outer ring are drawn into a stave basket in 1991 and 1992 weights. Since 1993, the design has changed each year, but all were made with a white lace ground. Weights made in 1993 have a center colored picture cane of a thistle sur- rounded by six amber canes that are elongated to form the petals of a flower. A spaced outer

PP47

Amethyst (1985)

Black (1986)

continued on next page

Ruby (1989)

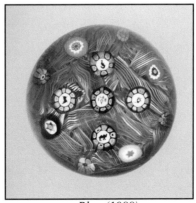

Blue (1988)

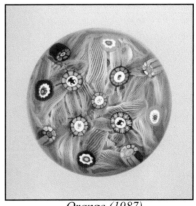

Orange (1987)

99

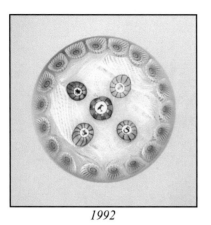

1992

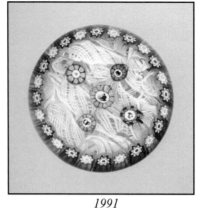

1991

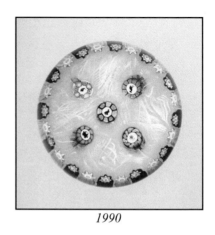

1990

1993

**PP47
(cont)**

ring contains three silhouette canes and three colored picture canes separated by complex millefiori canes. The 1994 design is similar to that of 1993, but has a pink flower. The 1995 design has a center silhouette or colored picture cane surrounded by a ring of five spaced complex canes and an outer ring of five silhouette or colored picture canes separated by twists. Weights made in 1996 have a blue lampwork flower and bud surrounded by a ring of canes that includes five silhouette or colored picture canes. The 1997 design has a center black and white picture cane of a bird surrounded by a garland of flowers and green leaves. Weights made in 1990 and thereafter are signed with a dated "P" cane in the base. Made 1981 - 1997. Limited edition.

1994

1995

1996

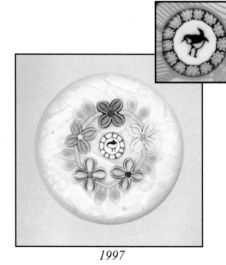

1997

*1981 - 1982,
1987 - 1994*

Old fashioned glass or tumbler (3-1/2 in. high, 3-1/4 in. dia.). The bottom contains a concentric millefiori pattern with five rings of canes surrounding a central "P" cane on a translucent blue ground. In 1992, a very small edition was made with a single pink or yellow lampwork flower with a center "P" cane replacing the millefiori pattern. Made 1981 - 1982 and 1987 - 1994.

PP48

1992

Medium millefiori weight with a complex center cane cluster consisting of a large center cane surrounded by four large canes and many closepacked smaller canes. Three pairs of spaced large canes surround this cluster. The perimeter of the weight has a garland-type ring that forms three large half-circles and three small half-circles, each of which contains a single large cane. The weight has a translucent color ground. Signed with a "P1982" cane in the base. Limited edition.

PP49

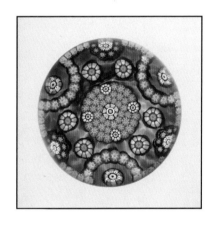

Large millefiori weight containing a center cane cluster with eight sets of three parallel twists radiating at an angle from it. Cane groups of 1-1-3-4 fill the area between the twists. The weight has a translucent color ground. Signed with a "P1982" cane in the base. Limited edition.

PP50

101

PP51   Not Issued

PP52   End-of-week bottle with matching stopper (5 in. high, 2-3/4 in. dia.). It contains crushed canes imbedded in either green, ruby or blue glass. Unsigned. Made 1982 - 1994.

PP53   Medium concentric millefiori weight with a pressed, fluted edge. The design consists of a center "P" cane surrounded by five rings of canes on a blue ground. Made 1982 - 1995.

Large weight containing a single red lampwork flower with ten or eleven petals and an equal number of green leaves on a black ground. Signed with a "P" cane in the base. Made 1983 only.

PP54

Not issued.

PP55

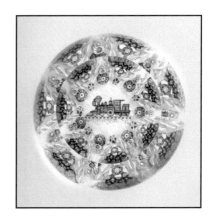

Large millefiori weight containing a glass transfer of a railway engine on a lace ground. A pattern of millefiori twists and canes forming a seven-pointed star surrounds the engine. The weight has a top facet. Signed with a "P" cane in the base. Made 1983 - 1988.

PP56

Millefiori inkwell with stopper (6 in. high, 4 in. dia.). The bottom contains a large butterfly made from millefiori canes and an outer ring of eight spaced millefiori canes on a translucent blue ground. The stopper also has a blue ground and contains a center "P" cane and eight spaced millefiori canes that match those in the bottom of the bottle. Made 1983 - 1984.

PP57

1983 - 1996

PP58

1997

Large millefiori weight with a pattern the same as the most recent PP1 design. However, while PP1 weights are domed, PP58 weights are faceted. Weights made through 1996 have a single top facet. Weights made in 1997 have a top facet and five side facets. The weight has a color ground. Signed with a "P" cane in the center of the setup. Made 1983 - 1997.

PP59

Medium millefiori weight with a pattern the same as the PP2 on a color ground. However, PP2 weights are domed, while PP59 weights have a single top facet. Signed with a "P" cane in the center of the setup. Made 1983 - 1997.

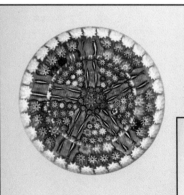

PP60

Medium millefiori weight with the same designs as the PP5. The weight has a translucent color ground and a single top facet. During the time the PP60 was made, the PP5 weights were not faceted. It is usually signed with a "P" cane in the center of the design. Made 1983 - 1995.

Other variations

 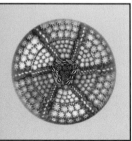

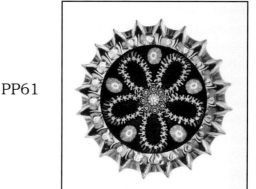

1983 - 1985

Medium millefiori weight with a pressed, fluted edge. Weights made from 1983 through 1985 have a central pattern of a five-pointed, curved star surrounded by five spaced millefiori canes on an opaque blue ground. In 1986 through 1988, weights were made with a pattern of five millefiori loops on an opaque blue ground. A concentric pattern on an opaque red ground was also produced in 1986 only. Most weights are signed with a center "P" cane, but a few are signed with a letter indicating the year it was made. Made 1983 - 1988.

PP61

1986 - 1988

1986

Large millefiori weight with a center "P" cane surrounded by three rings of canes and then sixteen short radial twists. The outer ends of the radials are separated by single millefiori canes. An outer ring of close millefiori canes completes the design. The weight has a color ground. Made 1983 - 1997.

PP62

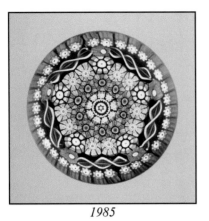

1985

1984

1983

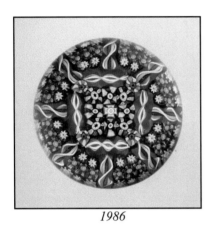

1986

PP63

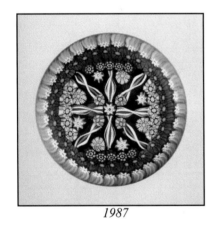

1987

Small millefiori weight with a translucent color ground. The complex patterns contain both large and small millefiori canes and twists and change each year. Signed with a dated "P" cane in the base. Made 1983 - 1996. Limited edition.

1988

1989

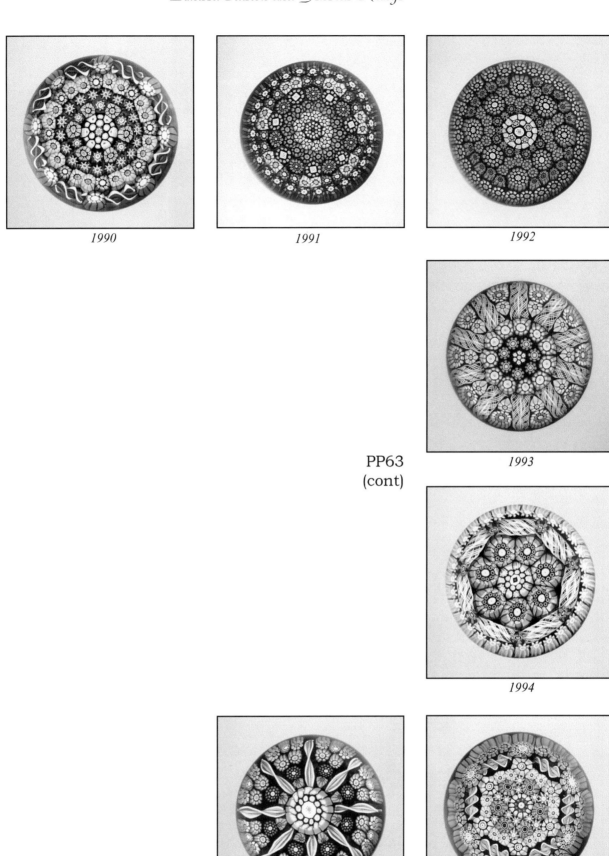

1990

1991

1992

PP63
(cont)

1993

1994

1996

1995

107

PP64

Medium concentric millefiori weight with a center complex cane surrounded by two rings of complex canes, then a ring of spaced canes, and an outer ring of close canes, all on a translucent color ground. Signed with a "P1983" cane in the base. Limited edition.

PP65

Large millefiori weight containing an eight-pointed millefiori star and two outer rings of canes, all on a translucent green or blue ground. Signed with a "P1983" cane in the base. Limited edition.

PP66

Clear ashtray or pin dish (4 in. dia.). It has a domed center that contains a blue lampwork flower on a white lace ground. Some are signed with a "P" cane at the base of the flower. Made 1983 only.

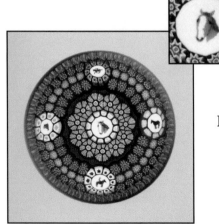

PP67

Medium concentric millefiori weight with a central colored picture cane of a horse's head and four other horse silhouette or colored picture canes on a translucent color ground. Signed with a "P" cane in the base. Made 1983 - 1984. Limited edition.

Medium millefiori weight with a central colored picture cane of a pheasant surrounded by a ring of canes and then by a four-pointed star that is outlined by twists. Cane groups of 4-3-2-1 fill in the points of the star, and four large canes are spaced around the star. The star points divide the outer cane ring into segments of eight canes each. The weight has a translucent color ground. Signed with a "P" cane in the base. Made 1983 - 1984. Limited edition.

PP68

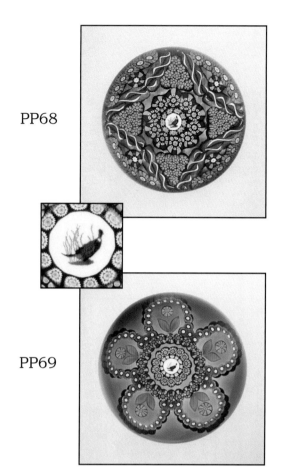

Large millefiori weight with a central colored picture cane of a pheasant. The center cane is surrounded by two rings of canes and five millefiori loops. Each loop encircles a "flower" cane and two leaves. The weight has a translucent, deep blue ground. Signed with a dated "P" cane in the base. Made 1983 - 1984. Limited edition.

PP69

Large swirl weight of white and a translucent color. Signed with a "P" cane in the base. Made 1984 - 1985.

PP70

Large complex concentric millefiori weight with a center group of four large canes and four short radial twists surrounded by two rings of canes. The ends of the twists divide the canes in the innermost ring into groups of four. A ring of twists and two outer rings of canes complete the design. The weight has a translucent color ground. Signed with a "P1984" cane in the base. Limited edition.

PP71

PP72

Large millefiori weight with a center complex cane surrounded by a ring of canes and then by ten short radial twists separating cane groups of 1-1-1. The canes in each group vary from small at the center to large at the outside. A ring of twists and an outer ring of canes complete the pattern. The weight has a translucent color ground. Signed with a "P1984" cane in the base. Limited edition.

PP73

Large doorknob with pressed, fluted edges. It has a concentric millefiori pattern with a center "P" cane surrounded by five rings of canes. It usually has a blue ground but a few were made with a red, green, or black ground. Made 1984 - 1997.

PP74

Large faceted bottle (6 in. high, 3-1/4 in. dia.). The bottom of the bottle has a complex center cane surrounded by a five-sided millefiori pattern, all on an opaque blue ground. The bottle has eight facets around the neck and five sets of three facets each near the bottom. The stopper contains a complex cane and has four large side facets and eight smaller facets around the top. Signed with a "P" in one of the outer canes in the bottom of the bottle. Made 1984 - 1985.

Miniature concentric millefiori weight with a center "P" cane surrounded by four rings of canes. The weight has a blue ground and pressed, fluted edges. Made 1985 - 1997.

PP75

Miniature concentric millefiori cupboard knob with a center "P" cane surrounded by four rings of canes. It has a blue ground and pressed, fluted edges. Made 1985 - 1997.

PP76

Medium open concentric millefiori weight with a center "P" cane surrounded by three rings of canes on a translucent ruby ground. The outermost ring includes six millefiori cane clusters. The weight has one top facet, six side facets, and a flat, star-cut base. Made 1985 only. Limited edition.

PP77

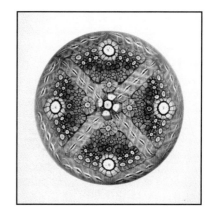

Large millefiori weight with four twists radiating from a center cane to form a cross that separates four cane groups. Each group has one large cane, then rows of medium canes in a 4-5-6 pattern, and an outer row with a large cane at the center and three smaller canes on each side. An outer ring of twists completes the design. The weight has a translucent color ground. Signed with a dated "P" cane in the base. Made 1985 - 1986. Limited edition.

PP78

PP79

Large millefiori weight with a center complex cane surrounded by four complex canes and eight radial twists separating cane groups of 1-2-3. An outer ring of millefiori canes is segmented by four of the twists. The weight has a translucent color ground. Signed with a "P1985" cane in the base. Limited edition.

PP80

Small translucent blue vase (4 in. high, 2-3/4 in. dia.) with vertical latticinio twists. Other colors were made as prototypes. Unsigned. Made 1985 only.

Large millefiori weight with several distinct designs. Weights made from 1985 through 1991 contain a center glass transfer of a golfer surrounded by three rings of twists and canes on a lace ground. Weights made in 1992 and thereafter feature a center colored picture cane of a golfer with golf clubs and have a translucent color ground. In the 1992 and 1993 design, the center cane is surrounded by a complex concentric pattern that is accented by six large canes near the perimeter. The 1994 weights feature large radial latticinio spokes separated by single large millefiori canes. Weights made in 1995 are similar, but the spokes are separated by a millefiori cane, a short twist, and a pair of canes. The design for 1997 is the same as the 1994 design. All weights are signed with a dated "P" cane in the base. Made 1985 - 1995 and 1997. Limited edition.

PP81

1995

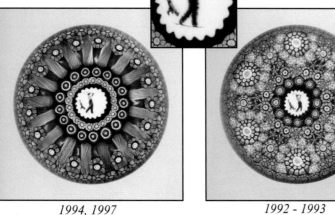

1994, 1997   *1992 - 1993*

1985 - 1991

112

Small dish (3 in. dia.) with a single large lamp-work flower on a translucent blue ground. Signed with a "P" cane near the flower. Flowers vary. Made 1985 only.

PP82

Large faceted millefiori inkwell made in two distinct styles. In both, the bottom of the bottle contains a large "P" cane surrounded by rings of canes and twists. Bottles made from 1985 through 1992 (7-1/2 in. high, 3-1/2 in. dia.) have eight rectangular facets around the top of the neck, eight small oval facets around the upper body, and eight large facets around the lower body. The stopper contains a pattern similar to that in the bottle and it has one top facet and eight side facets. The bottle has a large translucent blue foot. Bottles made in 1993 and thereafter are teardrop shaped (6-1/4 in. high, 2-1/4 in. dia.). There are three rows of six facets each around the body and the blue foot is much smaller. The stopper has a single lampwork flower with a "P" cane at the center on a translucent blue ground and has one top facet and six side facets. Made 1985 - 1997.

PP83

1985 - 1992

1993 - 1997

PP84

Large millefiori weight with a complex center cane surrounded by a ring of complex canes and eight radial twists that separate cane groups of 1-2-3 with the "1" being a very large cane. In some weights, a very small cane is added between the center ring and the large cane. The weight has a translucent color ground. Signed with a "P1986" cane in the base. Limited edition.

PP85

Large millefiori weight with a five-pointed star outlined by groups of three flattened colored rods each. Within the star, a complex center cane is surrounded by rings and groups of large and small millefiori canes, all on a color ground. Signed with a "P1986" cane in the base. Limited edition.

PP86

Medium complex millefiori weight with a large center cane cluster surrounded by a complex pattern of short twists and cane groups on a translucent color ground. Signed with a "P1986" cane in the base. Limited edition.

Large millefiori weight made in two distinct designs. Weights made from 1986 through 1988 have a glass transfer of a fisherman surrounded by three rings of twists and millefiori canes on a lace ground. The weight has a single top facet. This design was discontinued in 1989. In 1996, the weight was reintroduced with a colored picture cane of a fisherman surrounded by two rings of canes and then radial latticinio spokes separating groups of 1-twist-2, all on a translucent color ground. Weights made in 1997 have the same design. All weights are signed with a dated "P" cane in the base. Made 1986 - 1988 and 1996 - 1997. Limited edition.

PP87   *1986 - 1988*

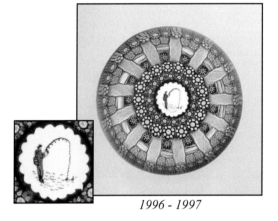

1996 - 1997

Large millefiori weight with a center cluster of millefiori canes surrounded by five similar clusters and an outer ring of millefiori canes on a dark color ground. Weights made in 1995 and thereafter have a dark blue ground. Signed with a "P" in the center cane cluster. Made 1987 - 1997.

PP88

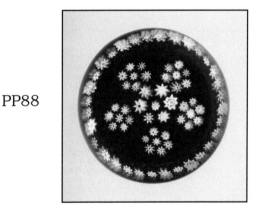

Medium millefiori weight with millefiori canes outlining a pentagon that is surrounded by a spaced ring of five large and five small canes and an outer close ring of canes on a dark ground. Signed with a "P" cane in the spaced ring. Made 1987 - 1990.

PP89

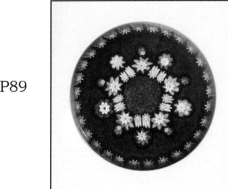

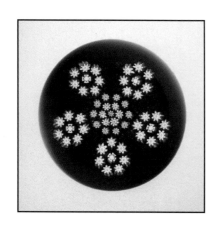

PP90

Medium millefiori weight with a center cane cluster surrounded by five smaller cane clusters on a dark ground. Signed with a "P" cane in the center cluster. Made 1987 - 1988.

PP91

Shot glass with a single lampwork flower on a translucent blue ground in the bottom (1-7/8 in. dia., 2-3/4 in. high). Unsigned. Made 1987 - 1988.

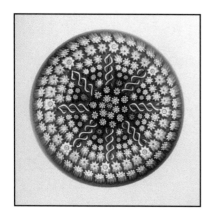

PP92

Large millefiori weight with a center "P" cane surrounded by two rings of canes, eight short radial twists separating cane groups of 1-2-3-3, and two outer rings of canes, all on a color ground. Made 1987 - 1993.

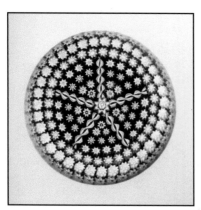

PP93

Large millefiori weight with a center "P" cane surrounded by five short radial twists separating cane groups of 1-2-3-4 and then by three outer rings of canes. The weight has a color ground. Made 1987 - 1990.

1996 - 1997

Large millefiori weight made in two distinct designs. Weights made from 1987 through 1992 have a center "P" cane surrounded by a ring of canes, then eight short radial twists separating cane groups of 1-1-2-3, then a ring of twists with eight spaced canes and an outer ring of canes, all on a color ground. In 1993, the design changed to two rings of canes surrounded by five radials that separate cane groups of 3-2-5 and extend through the ring of twists. The new design includes five pairs of canes that separate the radial twists from the twists in the ring. Made 1987 - 1997.

PP94

1996 - 1997

Large millefiori weight with a complex center cane surrounded by two rings of complex canes, then six short radial twists separating cane groups of 3-4, a hexagon of latticinio rods with millefiori canes at the corners, and an outer ring of canes, all on a translucent color ground. Signed with a "P1987" cane in the base. Limited edition.

PP95

Large millefiori weight with a complex center cane surrounded by a ring of canes and then four radial twists separating cane groups that include three rows of canes, a latticinio rod with a cane at each end, and then another row of canes. The canes in the groups are arranged in straight lines, resulting in a square pattern. The square pattern is surrounded by an outer ring divided by short twists into four segments of five canes each. The weight has a translucent color ground. Signed with a "P1987" cane in the base. Limited edition.

PP96

PP97

Large millefiori weight with a center complex cane surrounded by four large complex canes forming the inner corners of a Maltese cross that is outlined by twists. Cane groups of 1-2-3 are in the spaces between the arms of the cross, and pairs of cane groups of 1-1-1, separated by a radial twist, arc inside each of the arms. There is an outer ring of millefiori canes in groups of six alternating with short twists. The weight has a translucent color ground. Signed with a "P1987" cane in the base. Limited edition.

PP98

Medium millefiori weight with a complex center cane surrounded by a group of complex canes, then a ring of canes, a hexagon of six short, straight rods with a cane at each corner, and an outer ring of canes, all on a translucent color ground. Signed with a "P1987" cane in the base. Limited edition.

PP99

Medium millefiori weight with a complex center cane surrounded by four short radial twists separating cane groups of 1-3, then a close ring of canes and sixteen short radial twists separating cane groups of 1-1, all on a translucent color ground. Signed with a "P1987" cane in the base. Limited edition.

PP100

Medium millefiori weight with a center cane surrounded by five triangular cane groups of 1-2-3 that are outlined by twists. There are two outer cane rings. The weight has a translucent color ground. Signed with a "P1988" cane in the base. Limited edition.

118

Medium millefiori weight with a complex center cane surrounded by a close ring of complex canes, a ring of spaced small canes, and a narrow space. Then eight short radial twists, each with a single cane at the inner end, separate cane groups of 3-4-4, and an outer ring of twists completes the pattern. The weight has a translucent color ground. Signed with a "P1988" cane in the base. Limited edition.

PP101

Medium millefiori weight with a center cane surrounded by two close rings of canes and then a seven-pointed star outlined by fourteen short twists. A large cane is set inside the star points and a small cane is set at each inner point of the star. Cane groups of 1-3 are set between the star points, and an outer ring of seven large canes separated by short twists completes the pattern. The weight has a translucent color ground. Signed with a "P1988" cane in the base. Limited edition.

PP102

Large millefiori weight with a center cane surrounded by a ring of canes and then ten short radial twists that separate alternating cane groups of 1-2-2 and 1-1-1-1. A ring of short twists that alternate with segments of seven canes each and an outer ring of close millefiori canes complete the design. The weight has a translucent color ground. Signed with a "P1988" cane in the base. Limited edition.

PP103

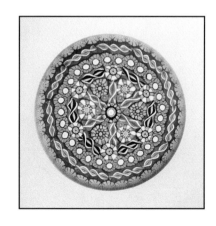

Large millefiori weight with a center cane surrounded by six short radial twists separating groups of one small and one large millefiori cane. A ring containing six millefiori canes alternating with short twists, a ring of close millefiori canes, a ring of twists, and an outer ring of close millefiori canes complete the design. The weight has a translucent color ground. Signed with a "P1988" cane in the base. Limited edition.

PP104

PP105

Large millefiori weight with a center cane surrounded by a ring of canes and then six short radial twists separating cane groups of 1-1-2-4. Another ring of six large complex canes alternating with short twists and an outer ring of close canes complete the design. The weight has a translucent color ground. Signed with a "P1988" cane in the base. Limited edition.

PP106

Large millefiori weight with a complex center cane that is surrounded by one ring of canes and is the center of a closepacked millefiori cross design. The ends of the cross arms are outlined by pairs of twists. Four complex cane groups, each dominated by a single very large cane, fill the areas between the cross points. The weight has a translucent color ground. Signed with a "P1988" cane in the base. Limited edition.

PP107

Small concentric millefiori weight, identical to the PP3, except for a colored picture cane of a butterfly in the center. Signed with a "P" cane in the base. Made 1989 - 1996.

PP108

Medium millefiori weight with a design similar to the PP2, except for a colored picture cane of a butterfly in the center. The weight has a color ground. Signed with a "P" cane in the base. Made 1989 - 1997.

Large millefiori weight, similar to the PP1, except for a colored picture cane of a butterfly in the center. The weight has a color ground. Signed with a "P" cane in the base. Made 1989 - 1997.

PP109

Medium concentric millefiori weight with a colored picture cane of a butterfly in the center surrounded by four rings of complex canes. The outer two rings are divided into six segments by short radial twists. The weight has a translucent color ground. Signed with a "P" cane in the base. Made 1988 - 1989. Limited edition.

PP110

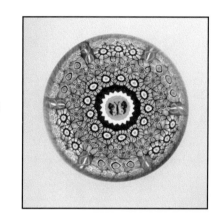

Medium millefiori weight with a center cane surrounded by two rings of canes, a ring of short radial twists, a ring of spaced canes, another ring of short twists, and an outer ring of spaced canes, all on a translucent color ground. Signed with a "P1989" cane in the base. Limited edition.

PP111

Medium millefiori weight with a large complex center cane surrounded by two rings of canes, a pentagon of millefiori canes and short twists, a pentagon of canes, and an outer pentagon of twists with two canes at each corner. The weight has a translucent color ground. Signed with a "P1989" cane in the base. Limited edition.

PP112

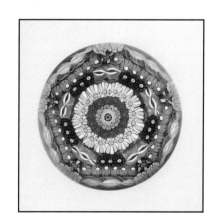

PP113

Medium millefiori weight with a large complex center cane and four radial twists that divide the weight into quarters. Each quarter contains a cane group of 2-3-5-5-8. An outer ring of canes completes the design. The weight has a translucent color ground. Signed with a "P1989" cane in the base. Limited edition.

PP114

Large millefiori weight with a complex center cane group and seven triangular sections formed by radial twists and an outer ring of twists on a translucent color ground. Each triangle contains a 1-1-twist-3 group. Signed with a "P" cane or a "P1989" cane in the base. Made 1989 only. Limited edition.

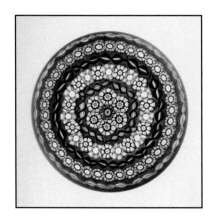

PP115

Large concentric millefiori weight with a center cane surrounded by three rings of canes alternating with three rings of twists on a translucent color ground. Signed with a "P1989" cane in the base. Limited edition.

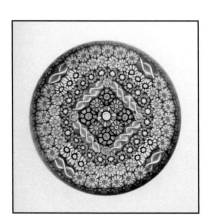

PP116

Large millefiori weight with a square center pattern formed by nine large canes and outlined by twists. This square is surrounded by two octagons of canes, a ring of canes accented by four short twists, and then an outer ring of canes. The weight has a translucent color ground. Signed with a "P1989" cane in the base. Limited edition.

Large millefiori weight with a center cane surrounded by two rings of canes and then six short radial twists that separate triangular groups of canes, each of which is dominated by one large cane. Two outer cane rings complete the pattern. The weight has a translucent color ground. Signed with a "P1989" cane in the base. Limited edition.

PP117

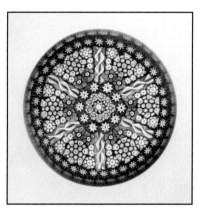

Small millefiori weight with a center cane surrounded by a close ring of six canes and a ring of six spaced canes on a mottled color ground. Signed with a "P" cane in the base. Made 1989 only.

PP118

Medium millefiori weight with an eight-pointed star filled in with canes on a dark ground. It was made with a deep blue ground each year and, in 1991 through 1994, it was also made with a black ground. Signed with a "P" cane in the center of the star. Made 1989 - 1997.

PP119

Medium millefiori weight with three curved lines of canes extending outward from a center "P" cane and joining an outer ring of canes. Three pairs of spaced complex canes are in the open areas between the curved lines. The weight has a color ground. Made 1989 only.

PP120

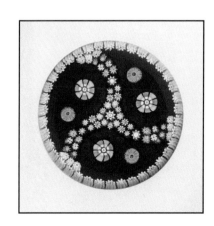

PP121

Medium complex millefiori weight with a large center colored picture cane of the head of a marmalade cat. The picture cane is made from more than 5000 individual glass rods. It is surrounded by a ring of canes, three pairs of large spaced canes, and an outer millefiori garland. The garland loops closely around three millefiori canes and contains three large half circles that curve inward. A large complex cane is in the center of each half circle. The weight was made with a ruby, blue, green, or red translucent ground. Signed with a "P" cane in the base. Made 1989 only. Limited edition.

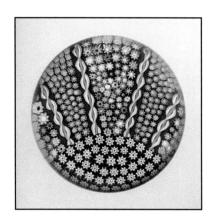

PP122

Large millefiori weight in the style of a sunrise. Four rays of twists, emanating from a cane group that represents the sun, divide the weight into wedges of millefiori canes on a color ground. Signed with a "P" cane in the center wedge. Made 1990 - 1995.

PP123

Small concentric millefiori weight with a large complex center cane surrounded by three rings of canes and a ring of twists on a color ground. Signed with a "P" cane in the base. Made 1990 - 1997.

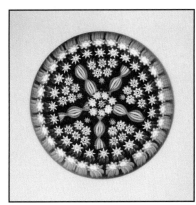

PP124

1990 - 1995

1996 - 1997

Small millefiori weight made in two distinct designs. Weights made from 1990 through 1995 have a center "P" cane surrounded by one ring of millefiori canes, five short radial twists separating cane groups of 1-2-3, and two outer rings of canes, all on a color ground. Weights made in 1996 and 1997 have six radials that extend to the edge of the weight. The radials separate cane groups of 1-2-3-4 that alternate with groups of 1-twist-4. Some weights made during the first years of the design are signed with a "P" cane in the base instead of in the design. Made 1990 - 1997.

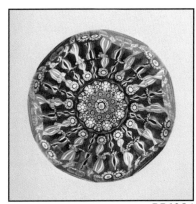

PP125

PP125A

Medium millefiori weight with a center cane surrounded by two rings of complex canes, then an open space, a ring of spaced millefiori canes alternating with short radial twists, and an outer ring of pairs of canes alternating with short radial twists. The weight has a translucent color ground. Signed with a "P1990" cane in the base. A version with a top facet and six side facets is designated PP125A. Limited edition.

PP126

PP126A

Medium complex millefiori weight with a center complex cane surrounded by four short radial twists separating cane groups of 1-2-5. An octagon formed by four twists alternating with four segments of three canes each, another octagon of four twists alternating with four segments of four canes each, and then an outer close ring of canes complete the pattern. The weight has a translucent color ground. Signed with a "P1990" cane in the base. A faceted version is designated PP126A. Limited edition.

PP127

Medium millefiori weight with a center cane surrounded by two rings of millefiori canes and then eight radial twists separating cane groups of 1-2-3-3 on a translucent color ground. Signed with a "P1990" cane in the base. A version with a top facet and six side facets is designated PP127A. Limited edition.

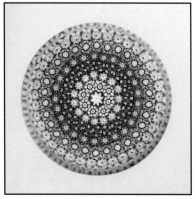

PP128

Large concentric millefiori weight with a center cane surrounded by seven close millefiori rings on a translucent color ground. Signed with a "P1990" cane in the base. A version with a top facet and six side facets is designated PP128A. Limited edition.

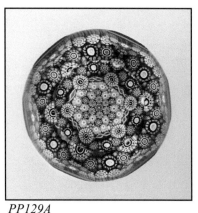

PP129A

PP129

Large concentric millefiori weight with a large center cane cluster, made up of a single cane and three tightly packed rings of canes. The cluster is surrounded by six large spaced complex millefiori canes alternating with short twists and then two outer rings that include both large and small canes. The weight has a translucent color ground. Signed with a "P1990" cane in the base. A version with a top facet and six side facets is designated PP129A. Limited edition.

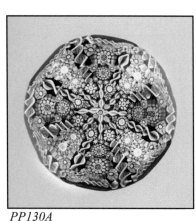

PP130A

PP130

Large millefiori weight with a center cane surrounded by four smaller canes. Four long and four short radial twists extend from this center cane group and separate cane groups of one small and one large cane. A second set of radial twists, offset from the first, extends from these cane groups to the outer ring and further separates cane groups of one large cane surrounded by two small and two medium canes. An outer ring of twists contains four large canes. The weight has a translucent color ground. Signed with a "P1990" cane in the base. A version with a top facet and six side facets is designated PP130A. Limited edition.

Large millefiori weight with a colored picture cane of a butterfly at the center surrounded by a ring of canes and then twists that outline a six-pointed star with 1-1 cane groups in the points. Between the star points are six cane groups of 1-2-4, each containing a silhouette or colored picture cane. An outer ring of canes completes the design. The weight has a translucent color ground. Signed with a "P1990" cane in the base. A version with a top facet and six side facets is designated PP131A. Limited edition.

PP131

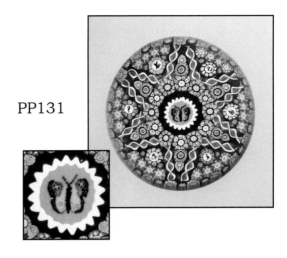

Large pear-shaped inkwell with a millefiori base and matching stopper (6 in. high, 3-1/2 in. dia.). The patterns in the bottle and the stopper are identical. They have a "P" cane at the center surrounded by a ring of millefiori canes and then six radial twists separating cane groups of one large, five medium, and four small canes, all on a color ground. There are eight facets around the upper body of the bottle and eight large facets around the lower body. The stopper has one top facet and six side facets. Made 1990 - 1994.

PP132

Pedestal rose weight (5-1/4 in. high, 2-3/4 in. dia.). It was made in ruby, blue, yellow, and amethyst. The weight has one top facet and six side facets. Unsigned. Made 1990 - 1993.

PP133

127

PP133A

Rose weight, similar to PP133, but without the pedestal. In 1993 it was made in ruby, blue, yellow, and amethyst. It was made in ruby, blue, and amethyst in 1994 and only in ruby and blue in 1995. It has one top facet and six side facets. Unsigned. Made 1993 - 1995.

PP134

Medium millefiori weight with a large complex cane and four small canes set in each quarter of a large square outlined and divided by twists. The large square is surrounded by a ring of complex canes that is divided into four segments by the radial twists. The weight has a translucent color ground. Signed with a "P1991" cane in the base. A version with a top facet and six side facets is designated PP134A. Limited edition.

PP135

Medium millefiori weight with a large complex center cane surrounded by a ring of canes, a ring of nine short radial twists separating cane groups of 1-1, and then two outer rings of canes. The weight has a translucent color ground. Signed with a "P1991" cane in the base. Limited edition.

Medium millefiori weight with a large center cluster consisting of a complex cane surrounded by two rings of canes. This cluster forms the center of a seven-pointed star that is formed by fourteen short twist segments. Cane groups of 1-1 fill the points of the star and cane groups of 1-2-3 separate the points of the star. An outer close ring of canes completes the design. The weight has a translucent color ground. Signed with a "P1991" cane in the base. A version with a top facet and six side facets is designated PP136A. Limited edition.

PP136

Large millefiori weight with a large center cane cluster consisting of a complex center cane surrounded by two rings of complex canes. The cluster is surrounded by fourteen radial twists separating cane groups of 1-1-1-1, increasing in size from the center outward. The weight has a translucent color ground. Signed with a "P1991" cane in the base. Limited edition.

PP137

Large millefiori weight with a large square outlined by twists. Within the square are rows of canes and a diamond formed by other twists. A ring of complex canes surrounds the complex square. The weight has a translucent color ground. Signed with a "P1991" cane in the base. Limited edition.

PP138

Large millefiori weight with a complex center cane surrounded by a ring of complex canes and then eight radial twists separating cane groups of 1-1-1-2, alternating with cane groups of 3-3-4-5 or 2-3-4-5. An outer ring of canes completes the design. The weight has a translucent color ground. Signed with a "P1991" cane in the base. A version with a top facet and six side facets is designated PP139A. Limited edition.

PP139

129

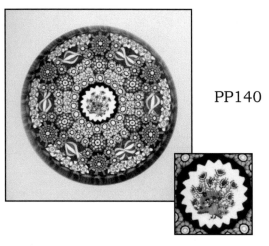

PP140

Magnum millefiori weight with a colored picture cane of a peacock in the center surrounded by three rings of canes and then a ring of six short twists alternating with half-round cane groups. The outer edges of the half-round groups are linked by groups of three canes each, and an outer ring of canes completes the design. The weight has a translucent color ground and a diameter of 3-1/4 inches. Signed with a "P1991" cane in the base. Limited edition.

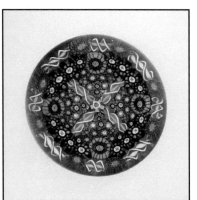

PP141

Medium complex millefiori weight with a central cross of four short twist canes separating triangular 1-3-4-4 groups of small and medium canes, all surrounded by a ring of canes highlighted by four large canes. An outer ring of eight large canes separated by four long twists alternating with four short twists completes the pattern. The weight has a translucent color ground. Signed with a "P1992" cane in the base. A faceted version is designated PP141A. Limited edition.

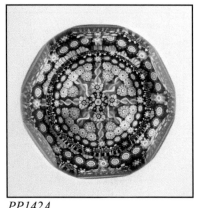

PP142A

PP142

Medium millefiori weight with a complex center cane surrounded by four short radial twists alternating with four large canes. Four additional radial twists extend outward from the four large canes, further separating the cane groups in the quadrants and dividing a surrounding ring into four groups of five canes each. Two outer rings of canes complete the pattern. The weight has a translucent color ground. Signed with a "P1992" cane in the base. A faceted version is designated PP142A. Limited edition.

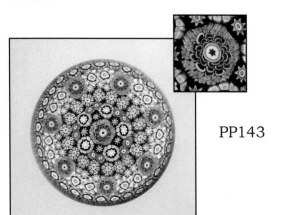

PP143

Medium concentric millefiori weight with a large pompon cane at the center surrounded by five rings of complex canes, all on a translucent color ground. Seven additional pompon canes are spaced within the fourth ring. Signed with a "P1992" cane in the base. Limited edition.

Large concentric millefiori weight with a complex center cane surrounded by a ring of four large, four medium, and eight small complex canes and then a ring of twelve short radial latticinio rods separating cane groups of 1-2. Six outer short radial latticinio rods separate two outer rings of canes into groups of 3-4. The weight has a translucent color ground. Signed with a "P1992" cane in the base. Limited edition.

PP144

Large complex millefiori weight with three short radial twists and three longer radial latticinio rods extending from a complex center cane and dividing the weight into six triangular cane groups. Three cane groups of 1-2-3-4-4 alternate with another three groups, each of which contains a silhouette or black and white picture cane surrounded by three small canes and then two rows of four canes each. Three pompon canes are near the outer edge of the weight. An outer ring of latticinio rods alternating with millefiori canes completes the design. The weight has a translucent color ground. Signed with a "P1992" cane in the base. Limited edition.

PP145

Large millefiori weight with twist canes outlining five squares set in a cross form and four radial twists extending from the corners of the center square to the edge of the weight. The center square contains a square arrangement of one large and twelve small canes. Each of the four side squares contains one large complex cane. Each corner of each square is accented by a single cane. Cane groups of 1-1-2-3 are set in the spaces around the outer squares. The weight has a translucent color ground. Signed with a "P1992" cane in the base. A faceted version is designated PP146A. Limited edition.

PP146

PP146A

131

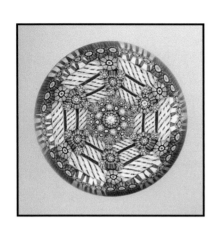

PP147

Magnum millefiori weight with a hexagonal pattern. The center six-sided cane group consists of a complex cane surrounded by two rings of canes. Three concentric six-sided rings of latticinio rods are accented by radials formed by millefiori canes at the corners. A large complex cane dominates each of these six radials and an outer cane ring completes the design. The weight has a translucent color ground. It has a diameter of 3-1/4 inches. Signed with a "P1992" cane in the base. Limited edition.

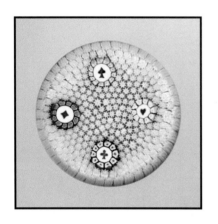

PP148

Medium millefiori weight containing heart, diamond, club, and spade silhouette canes on a carpet set above a translucent color ground. Some of the silhouettes are made with translucent colored glass. Signed with a "P" cane in the base. Made 1992 only.

PP149

Medium millefiori weight laid out in a cruciform pattern. The center cane group has a large complex center cane, four large pompon canes, and four other complex canes placed to form a square. Four twists, outlined by canes, form the arms of the cross. Wedges of stardust canes in a 1-2-3 pattern fill the area between the cross arms. The weight has a translucent color ground. Signed with a "P1993" cane in the base. Limited edition.

PP150

Medium concentric millefiori weight with a center complex cane surrounded by two rings of canes, then a ring of twists, another ring of canes, and an outer ring of twists, all on a translucent color ground. Signed with a "P1993" cane is in the base. Limited edition.

Medium millefiori weight with four short radial twists extending from the center cane and joining four short twists set at right angles to form a square with four quarters. Each quarter contains a cane group of 1-2. The square is further accented by a large complex cane at each of the four corners. Four segments of five canes each are placed between the large corner canes to complete a ring. An outer ring of canes completes the pattern. The weight has a translucent color ground. Signed with a "P1993" cane in the base. A version with a top facet and six side facets is designated PP151A. Limited edition.

PP151

Large faceted millefiori weight with a center cane surrounded by six short radial latticinio rods alternating with six canes, then by a ring of close canes and a ring of sixteen radial latticinio rods alternating with single canes placed near the outer edge. An outer ring of canes completes the pattern. The weight has a translucent color ground of ruby, blue, or green. It has one top facet and six side facets. Signed with a "P1993" cane in the base. Limited edition.

PP152

Large complex millefiori weight with a center cane surrounded by a ring of canes and then by four groups of one large and two small canes alternating with diamonds that are outlined by short twists. Each diamond contains a large cane and two small canes. Four semicircular cane groups, each containing a large, complex cane, are placed between the diamonds at the outer edge of the weight. Segments of seven canes each connect these groups to form an outer ring. The weight has a translucent color ground. Signed with a "P1993" cane in the base. A version with a top facet and six side facets is designated PP153A. Limited edition.

PP153

133

PP154

Large millefiori weight containing nine silhouette or picture canes laid out to form a square. The center picture cane is surrounded by a ring of canes. Additional canes are closely packed to fill the spaces between the silhouette and picture canes. A short twist is set at the outer edge of each side of the square. Two close concentric rings of complex canes complete the pattern. The weight has a translucent color ground. Signed with a "P1993" cane in the base. Limited edition.

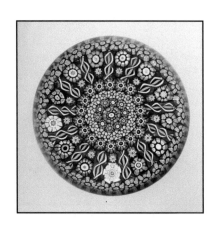

PP155

Magnum millefiori weight arranged in a "wagon wheel" design. A complex center cane is surrounded by three rings of canes, then thirteen short radial twists forming the wheel spokes and separating cane groups of one small and one large cane. An outer ring of canes forms the rim of the wheel. The weight has a translucent color ground and a diameter of 3-1/4 inches. Signed with a "P1993" cane in the base. Limited edition.

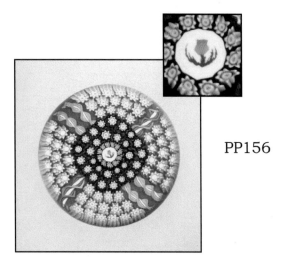

PP156

Medium millefiori weight with a center colored picture cane of a thistle surrounded by five rings of canes. Short radial twists separate the three outer rings of canes into four cane groups of 4-5-6. Two of the four radials are single twists and two are pairs of twists. The weight has a color ground. Signed with a "P" cane in the base. Made 1994 - 1997.

1995 - 1996

Small millefiori weight with a center colored picture cane of a thistle. Weights made in 1995 and 1996 have four radial twists that separate cane groups of 2-3-4-5 (or 6). Weights made in 1997 have five concentric rings and no radial twists. All have a color ground. Made 1995 - 1997. Signed with a "P" cane in the base.

PP156A

1997

Medium millefiori weight with a small center cane surrounded by a ring of small canes and then a ring of eight large canes. Eight radial twists then separate alternating cane groups of 1-3-3 and 1-twist-3, all on a translucent color ground. Signed with a "P1994" cane in the base. A version with a top facet and six side facets is designated PP157A. Limited edition.

PP157

Medium concentric millefiori weight with a large complex center cane surrounded by four large canes separating cane groups of 2-3. Ten short radial twists then separate cane groups of 2-1 with the outer cane being larger. A close ring of canes completes the design. The weight has a translucent color ground. Signed with a "P1994" cane in the base. Limited edition.

PP158

135

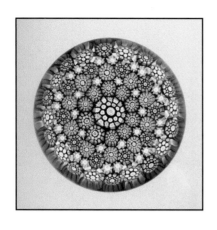

PP159

Medium concentric millefiori weight with a center cane surrounded by a close ring of large canes, then a spaced ring of small canes, a close ring of large canes, a spaced ring of pairs of small canes and an outer close ring of large canes, all on a translucent color ground. Signed with a "P1994" cane in the base. Limited edition.

PP160

Large millefiori weight with a complex center cane surrounded by a ring of canes, a ring of six short twists alternating with single canes, another ring of canes, and then thirteen short radial twists that separate cane groups of 1-1-twist, all on a translucent blue, ruby, or green ground. The weight has a top facet and six side facets. Signed with a "P1994" cane in the base. Limited edition.

PP161

Large millefiori weight with a center cane surrounded by a close ring of canes, two hexagons of canes, a hexagon of twists with millefiori canes at the corners, and then twelve radial twists separated by 1-1 cane groups alternating with single large canes. An outer ring of canes completes the pattern. The weight has a translucent color ground. Signed with a "P1994" cane in the base. A version with a top facet and six side facets is designated PP161A. Limited edition.

PP162

Large millefiori weight with a center cane surrounded by a ring of canes, seven short radial twists separating cane groups of 1-1-2, and then a ring of seven large silhouette or colored picture canes alternating with twists. The silhouette or picture canes also divide a ring of canes into segments of three canes each. An outer ring of pairs of canes alternating with short twists completes the design. The weight has a translucent color ground. Signed with a "P1994" cane in the base. Limited edition.

Small pressed concentric weight with a center "P" cane surrounded by four rings of canes on a blue ground. The weight has six pairs of pressed points. Made 1995 - 1997.

PP163

Medium millefiori weight with a center cane surrounded by a square of canes and then a group of four canes on each side of the square. Short twists outline four squares adjacent to the center square. Each of these squares contains a large complex cane and has a smaller cane at each corner. Cane groups of 2-4-5-5 are placed between the outer squares. Additional short radial twists extend from the corners of the center square into the cane groups. The weight has a translucent color ground. Signed with a "P1995" cane in the base. Limited edition.

PP164

Medium millefiori weight with a stardust center cane surrounded by a ring of yellow stardust canes and a ring of pink stardust canes, an open space, and then eight short radial twists separating cane groups of 2-2. An outer ring of latticinio rods alternating with pairs of canes completes the design. The weight has a translucent color ground. Signed with a "P1995" cane in the base. Limited edition.

PP165

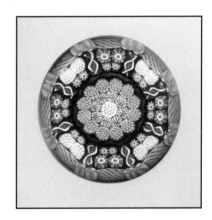

Medium millefiori weight with a large complex center cane surrounded by a ring of canes and then another ring with six pairs of small canes alternating with single large canes. The large canes are at the inner points of a six-pointed star outlined by twists. The points of the star are filled with cane groups of 2-1-1 and the spaces between the points are filled with cane groups of 1-2-4 alternating with groups of 1-3-4. The weight has a translucent color ground. Signed with a "P1995" cane in the base. A version with a top facet and six side facets is designated PP166A. Limited edition.

PP166

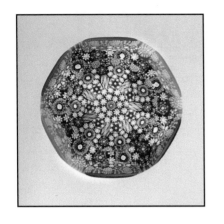

PP167

Large millefiori weight with a center cane surrounded by two rings of canes, seven short radial latticinio rods alternating with single large canes, and seven half-circles of canes alternating with large canes. A single large cane is placed in each half circle. An outer ring of canes completes the design, all on a translucent ruby, blue, or green ground. The weight has a top facet and six side facets. Signed with a "P1995" cane in the base. Limited edition.

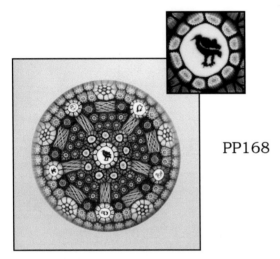

PP168

Large millefiori weight with a center black and white picture cane of a bird. The picture cane is surrounded by a ring of canes, then five short radial latticinio rods separating cane groups of 3-4, and then a ring of short rods and canes with a large silhouette or black and white picture cane at the outer end of each radial rod. Two outer rings of canes complete the design. Seven large canes divide both of these rings. The weight has a translucent color ground. Signed with a "P1995" cane in the base. Limited edition.

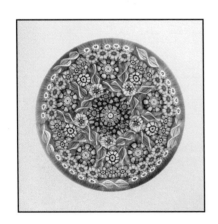

PP169

Large millefiori weight with a complex center cane surrounded by a ring of canes and five short twists alternating with large canes. Two twists extending outward from each of these large canes are separated by cane groups of 1-1-2 and a large cane is placed between each pair of twists. A close ring of canes and an outer ring of short twists alternating with five segments of five canes each completes the design. The weight has a translucent color ground. Signed with a "P1995" cane in the base. A version with a top facet and five side facets is designated PP169A. Limited edition.

PP170

1996

Small pressed millefiori weight with a center "P" cane surrounded by a ring of canes, six radial twists alternating with single canes, and then an outer ring of canes, all on a blue ground. Although Perthshire's 1996 catalogue shows eight radial twists, all weights were made with only six. Weights made in 1996 have twelve pressed scallops and weights made in 1997 have eight pressed scallops. Made 1996 - 1997.

1997

Medium pressed millefiori weight with a center "P" cane surrounded by a ring of canes and then six radial twists separating cane groups of 1-2-3-3 alternating with groups of 1-2-3-4, all on a color ground. Made 1996 - 1997.

PP171

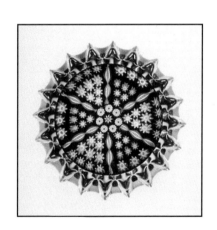

Medium millefiori weight with a center cane surrounded by a ring of canes, six radial twists separating 1-1-2-4 groups of large and small canes, and an outer ring of short twists alternating with segments of four canes each. The weight has a translucent color ground. Signed with a "P1996" cane in the base. A version with a top facet and six side facets is designated PP172A. Limited edition.

PP172

139

PP173

Medium millefiori weight with a center cane surrounded by two rings of canes, fourteen latticinio rods separating cane groups of 1-1, and an outer ring of canes, all on a translucent color ground. Signed with a "P1996" cane in the base. Limited edition.

PP174

Large millefiori weight with a center cane surrounded by four radial pink and white latticinio rods separating cane groups of 2-3-4. Offset from these radials are four radials, each consisting of two latticinio rods separated by three daisy canes. These radials extend from the inner cane groups to the edge of the weight. The spaces remaining between the pairs of radials are filled with cane groups of 2-2-5-6, with the inner radials further dividing the 2-2 parts of the groups. The weight has a translucent ruby, blue, or green ground. Signed with a "P1996" cane in the base. Limited edition.

PP175

Large millefiori weight with a center cane surrounded by two rings of canes, twelve radials separating cane groups of 1-1-2, and an outer ring of canes on a translucent ruby, blue, or green ground. Signed with a "P1996" cane in the base. A version with a top facet and six side facets is designated PP175A. Limited edition.

PP176

Large millefiori weight with a complex center cane surrounded by a ring of half-canes, twelve or thirteen short radial latticinio rods separating cane groups of 1-1-1, another ring of half-canes, and two outer rings of canes on a translucent blue, ruby, or green ground. The weight has a top facet and six side facets. Signed with a "P1996" cane in the base. Limited edition.

Magnum millefiori weight with a pink lampwork flower surrounded by five short radial twists separating cane groups of 4-3-4, then a ring of canes divided into segments of three canes each by short twists, and an outer ring of canes. The weight has a translucent amethyst-blue ground. It has a diameter of 3-1/4 inches. Signed with a "P1996" cane in the base. Limited edition.

PP177

Medium closepacked millefiori weight with simple canes on a color ground. Signed with a "P" cane in the setup. Made 1997.

PP178

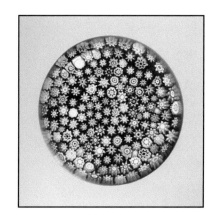

Small closepacked millefiori weight with simple canes on a color ground. Signed with a "P" cane in the setup. Made 1997.

PP178A

Medium millefiori weight with a complex center cane surrounded by a ring of canes, nine radial latticinio rods separating cane groups of 1-1, a ring of canes, a ring of latticinio rods, and an outer ring of canes, all on a translucent color ground. The weight has a top facet and six side facets. Signed with a "P1997" cane in the base. Limited edition.

PP179

PP180

Medium millefiori weight with a complex center cane surrounded by a ring of canes, eight short radial twists separating cane groups of 1-1, and then a ring of florets alternating with large canes that have a small cane on either side. An outer ring of twists alternating with canes completes the design. The weight has a translucent color ground. Signed with a "P1997" cane in the base. A version with a top facet and six side facets is designated PP180A. Limited edition.

PP181

Medium millefiori weight with a center ruby lampwork flower and buds surrounded by eleven short radial twists separating cane groups of 2-2-2 and then by an outer ring of canes, all on a white lace ground. The weight has a top facet and five side facets. Signed with a "P1997" cane in the base. Limited edition.

PP182

Large millefiori weight with a complex center cane surrounded by three rings of canes, seven pairs of radial twists separating cane groups of 2-2-3-4, and an outer ring of canes, all on a translucent color ground. Signed with a "P1997" cane in the base. A version with a top facet and seven side facets is designated PP182A. Limited edition.

PP183

Large millefiori weight with a complex center cane surrounded by three close rings of canes and then three rings of canes that are divided into segments of two or three canes each by short radial latticinio rods that extend across either the fourth and fifth rings or the fifth and sixth rings. An outer ring of canes completes the design. The weight has a translucent color ground. Signed with a "P1997" cane in the base. Limited edition.

Magnum millefiori weight with a center lamp-work butterfly with millefiori cane wings. The butterfly is surrounded by nine radial latticinio rods separating cane groups of 2-2-2 and a short twist with a cane on either side, all on a translucent color ground. The weight has a top facet and eight side facets. It has a diameter of 3-1/4 inches. Signed with a "P1997" cane in the base. Limited edition.

PP184

Large millefiori weight with a colored picture cane of a soccer player surrounded by two rings of canes and then thirteen radial latticinio spokes separating cane groups of 1-twist-2. An outer ring of canes completes the design. The weight has a translucent color ground. Signed with a "P1997" cane in the base. Limited edition.

PP185

143

Special Editions

Dated

RYDER CUP
Two blue golf clubs and a complex cane containing "USA GB" surrounded by a ring of canes on a lace ground. Signed with a "P1971" cane in the base. Produced specially for the Ryder Cup golf tournament. Edition size: 50.

1971

ISLE OF MAN
Three lines of canes spiraling outward from the center to meet a ring of canes around the outside, all on an opaque color ground. Signed with a "P1979" cane in the base.

1979

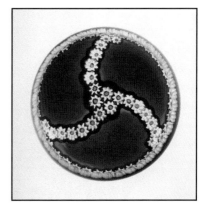

ROYAL WEDDING CROWN
A large colored picture cane of the Royal Wedding Crown and the date "29.7.81" set at the center of a crown of dark red-brown, white, and blue twists. Signed with a "P1981" cane in the base. Edition size: 145/136 made.

1981

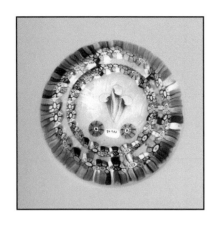

1981

ROYAL WEDDING FEATHERS
Miniature weight with three golden feathers symbolizing the Prince of Wales, a plaque with the date "29.7.81" set between two millefiori canes with wedding bells at their centers, and a millefiori cane garland, all on a white lace ground. One top facet. Signed with a "P" cane in the base. Edition size: 288/283 made.

1985

SMITHSONIAN
A special center complex cane surrounded by five latticinio radials dividing cane groups of 1-2-3-4 and an outer ring of latticinio rods. Produced exclusively for the Smithsonian Institution. Signed with a "P1985" cane in the base. Edition size: 500.

1986

ROYAL WEDDING
The "White Rose of York" on a translucent red ground with the date "23.7.86" in script, in commemoration of the wedding of His Royal Highness Prince Andrew and Miss Sarah Ferguson. One top facet and six side facets. Signed with a "P" cane in the base. A preproduction brochure indicated that this weight would not be made after 15 July 1986. Edition size: 300/132 made.

1987

COUNCIL TREE 1
A center colored picture cane of a large tree surrounded by a ring of canes and then eight radial twists separating cane groups of 1-2-3-3 on a translucent color ground. Signed with a "P1987" cane in the base. Produced exclusively for the Bergstrom-Mahler Museum. Edition size: 243/243 made.

ICE SKATER
A glass transfer of an ice skater surrounded by a ring of seven pairs of canes alternating with short twists and then by two rings of canes on a lace ground. One top facet. Produced exclusively for L.H. Selman Ltd. Signed with a "P1988" cane in the base. Only about 40 were made.

1988

FRENCH REVOLUTION 1
A large weight with a center colored picture cane of two crossed French flags surrounded by pattern of millefiori canes and twists on a translucent color ground. A large cane near the outer edge contains the dates "1789" and "1989." Two outer circles of canes complete the pattern. Signed with a "P" cane in the base. Edition size: 200/39 made.

1989

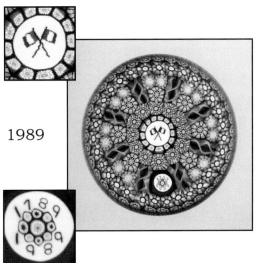

FRENCH REVOLUTION 2
A medium weight similar to FRENCH REVOLUTION 1, but with one outer circle of canes. It also has a cane with the dates "1789" and "1989." Signed with a "P" cane in the base. Edition size: 200/61 made.

1989

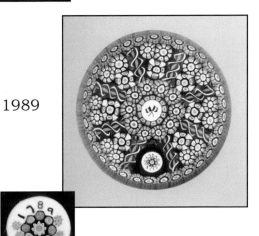

FRENCH REVOLUTION 3
A large weight with a center colored picture cane of two crossed French flags and a ring including five spaced complex millefiori canes and a large cane containing the dates "1789" and "1989." A cane garland completes the design. Set on a lace ground. Signed with a "P" cane in the base. Edition size: 200/37 made.

1989

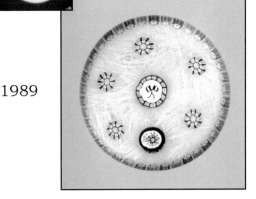

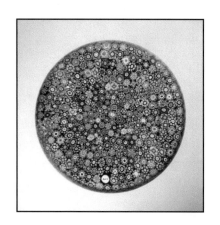

1992

MAGNUM CLOSEPACK
A magnum closepacked millefiori design containing complex canes. Faceted or domed. Signed "P1992" and "PM^cD" (for the maker, Peter McDougall) in canes within the design. Edition size: 50/50 made.

1995

CAMBRIDGE PAPERWEIGHT CIRCLE
A purple pasque flower on a stem with leaves on a clear ground. One top facet, six side facets, and a star-cut base. Signed "CPC 1995" in a cane next to the stem. Edition size: 40/40 made.

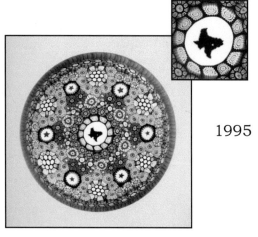

1995

TEXAS PCA
A large center picture cane with the state of Texas in black, except for a small white star representing Austin, the state capitol. The picture cane is surrounded by two rings of canes and a closepacked arrangement of large and small canes featuring six canes with a silhouette of a star. Cane colors vary. The weight has a translucent red ground. Signed with a "P1995" cane in the base. Made exclusively for The European Influence in conjunction with the Texas Paperweight Collectors Association. Edition size: 40/40 made.

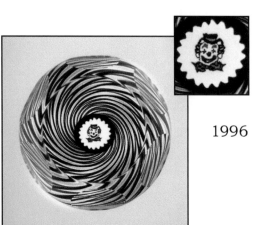

1996

CLOWN
A large colored picture cane of a clown's head at the center of a swirl of brown, white, and yellow on a translucent amethyst core. One top facet and six side facets. Signed "P1996" in a cane in the base. Edition size: 75/75 made.

PAPERWEIGHT COLLECTORS ASSOCIATION
A miniature weight with a complex center cane that contains the letters "P," "C," and "A" in individual canes. The center cane is surrounded by three rings of canes. Set on a translucent blue ground. Twenty pressed flutes around the edge. Signed with a "P1997" cane in the base. Edition size: 500/500 made.

1997

Undated

BERGSTROM-MAHLER CHRISTMAS TREE
A Christmas tree of closepacked millefiori canes with a yellow stardust cane at the top surrounded by a millefiori garland, all on a translucent red ground. Signed with a "P" cane in the trunk of the tree and scratch-signed "BMM" with the edition number on the base. Made exclusively for the Bergstrom-Mahler Museum. Edition size 50/50 made.

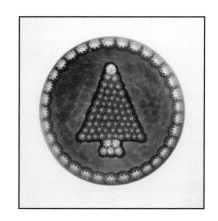

PAPERWEIGHT TOUR
A pattern of millefiori canes and twists similar to the first PP1 design. The weight has a large center cane with the letters "PT." Given as gifts to the participants of a Paperweight Tour when they visited the Perthshire factory in 1972. Some are signed "P1972" in canes in the base. Only about 25 were made.

GINGHAM WEIGHT

A magnum weight with a bouquet of five lamp-work flowers at the center, encased in a red-over-white double overlay, which has been cut in the traditional "gingham" pattern made famous by the antique St. Louis "gingham" weight. The "gingham" overlay is further encased in a heavy layer of clear crystal. One top facet. Signed with a "P" cane in the base or unsigned. Made in 1983. Edition size: 20/20 made.

SPANISH ARMADA

A center colored picture cane of a Spanish galleon surrounded by a pattern of millefiori canes and twists. One cane in the surrounding pattern contains a "400" indicating the 400th Anniversary of the Spanish Armada. Signed with a "P" cane in the base. Made in 1988. Edition size: 300/256 made.

25TH ANNIVERSARY

Pink complex canes and cane clusters all set around a pink three-dimensional flower on a translucent blue ground. One top facet and six side facets. Signed "P25" in a cane in the base. Made in 1993 to commemorate Perthshire's 25th Anniversary. Edition size: 200/200 made.

STATE BIRD

A center colored picture cane of an Eastern Bluebird, Chickadee, Quail, or Roadrunner surrounded by three rings of canes, all within a double overlay, which is further encased in clear crystal. Cane colors and outside overlay colors vary. Faceting on the overlay and on the clear encasement varies. Each piece is different. Signed with a "P" cane in the base. Only nineteen Eastern Bluebird weights, sixteen Chickadee weights, fourteen Quail weights, and six Roadrunner weights were made.

ENCASED DOUBLE OVERLAY
A magnum weight containing a lampwork bouquet on a translucent color ground within a double overlay, which is faceted and further encased in clear crystal, which is also faceted. Overlay colors vary. Faceting on the overlay and on the outside encasement varies and is intricate. Signed with a "P" cane in the base. No two are alike.

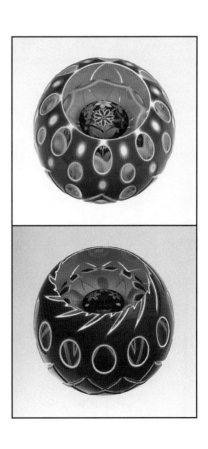

DOUBLE OVERLAY ENCASED DOUBLE OVERLAY
A lampwork bouquet on a translucent color ground within a double overlay, which is faceted and then encased in clear crystal and then in another double overlay. Overlay colors vary. Faceting on the inside and outside overlays varies and is intricate. No two are alike.

151

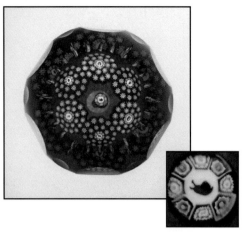
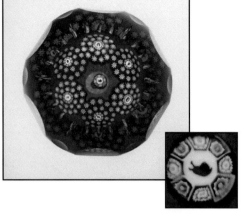

ART INSTITUTE

A center colored picture cane of a snail surrounded by six circlets, each containing a center silhouette or picture cane surrounded by two rings of canes, all on a translucent blue ground within a blue flash overlay. Circlet colors alternate between red and green. One top facet, six side facets, multiple flutes and a feathered edge around the top. Designed in association with the Art Institute of Chicago. Signed with a "P" cane in the base. Edition size: 200.

COUNCIL TREE 2

A miniature weight with a center colored picture cane of a tree surrounded by six radial twists that separate cane groups of 1-2-3, and then by an outer ring of twists, all on a translucent blue ground. Produced exclusively for the Bergstrom-Mahler Museum. Signed with a "P" cane in the base. Made in 1991.

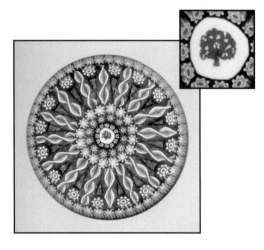

COUNCIL TREE 3

A large colored picture cane of a tree surrounded by two rings of canes, then twists separating single canes, and finally an outer ring of canes, all on a translucent green ground. Cane colors vary. Produced exclusively for the Bergstrom-Mahler Museum. Signed with a "P" cane in the base. Made in 1996.

SWAN BOAT

A gold "Swan Boat" surrounded by a ring of six pairs of canes alternating with short twists and three rings of close canes on a black ground. Made exclusively for a Boston jewelry store. Signed with a "P" cane in the base. Only 50 were made.

CROSS

Yellow stardust canes forming a cross surrounded by a ring of blue and white canes on a
translucent blue ground. Produced exclusively
for L. H. Selman Ltd. Signed with a "P" cane
in the base.

STAR OF DAVID

White stardust canes forming a Star of David
surrounded by a ring of light pink canes on a
translucent blue ground. Produced exclusively
for L. H. Selman Ltd. Signed with a "P" cane
in the base.

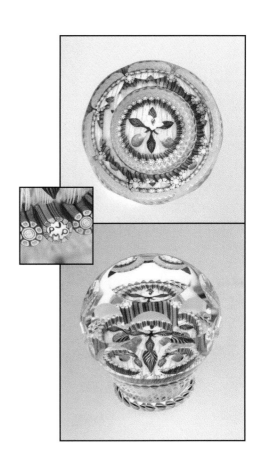

PERTHSHIRE/PARSLEY PEDESTAL

A collaborative weight made by Perthshire Paperweights and American artist, Johne Parsley.
It contains two pears, a white flower and four
green leaves surrounded by a ring of millefiori
canes on a ground of parallel latticinio strips.
The pedestal consists of a forty-strand latticinio basket bordered both top and bottom
by a white, pink, and blue torsade. One top
facet and sixteen side facets. Signed with a
"JPPM" cane (for the artists, Johne Parsley and
Peter McDougall) in the ring. The letters are
arranged in such a way that a "PP" signature
is also formed. Made in 1993. Edition size:
35/35 made.

NEW ORLEANS
A pink lampwork flower and two buds with a millefiori cane on each side of the stem and "New Orleans La" in white script lettering on a translucent blue ground. Top facet and six side facets. Made exclusively for a New Orleans gift shop. Signed with a "P" cane in the base.

CROWN NEWEL POST
A magnum crown with twists of red, green, and white alternating with white latticinio rods mounted on a brass fitting for attachment to a stair post. Unsigned.

MILLEFIORI CLOSEPACK NEWEL POST
A magnum round millefiori closepack mounted on a brass fitting for attachment to a stair post. Signed with a "PMᶜD" cane (for Peter McDougall, the maker).

Paperweight-related Items

BOWL
A bowl with latticinio cane sides and a closepacked millefiori pattern on a blue color ground in the bottom. Signed with a "P" cane within the design.

EARRINGS
A center cane surrounded by a ring of canes on a color ground attached to earring posts or clips. Colors vary.

MARBLE
Sphere of millefiori canes and pieces mixed with a dark colored glass. The sphere has a flattened base. Marbles made in the early 1990s have canes that are more complex than those in later marbles, which tend to be simple.

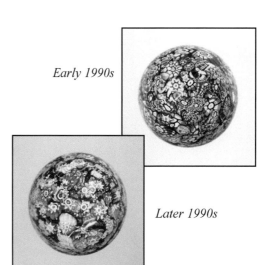

Early 1990s

Later 1990s

155

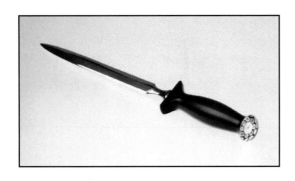

PAPER KNIFE (LETTER OPENER)

A single enclosed complex cane on a color ground attached to the black handle of a letter opener. Made 1988 - 1989.

Perthshire purchased 500 paper knife handles in 1988 and made paper knives until the supply of handles was used up. Some of the handles were used to make special orders. Thirty-six paper knives featuring a colored picture cane of the Council Tree were made for the Bergstrom-Mahler Museum. Also, approximately 100 paper knives with a purple handle and a special flower cane were made for a private firm.

Typical paper knife cane

Bergstrom-Mahler cane

PENDANT

A lampwork bouquet in a clear circular plaque held all around by gold wire to form a pendant. Made 1983 - 1984.

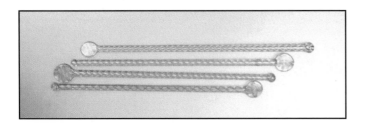

SWIZZLE STICK

Cane twist about 6 to 10 inches long with one end rounded and the other end flattened.

One-of-a-kind Weights

*Bouquet and latticinio
on red cushion (1995)*

*Double overlay encased
triple overlay (1980)*

Bouquet with flash overlay (1989)

*Encased mushroom with
millefiori ring (1977)*

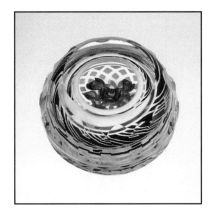

*Rose bouquet with black and white
double overlay (1982)*

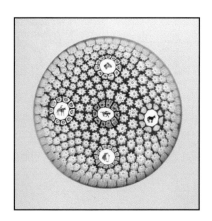

*Carpet ground with horse
picture canes (1995)*

Bouquet with double overlay (1989)

Butterfly with encased double overlay (1980)

Flower with double overlay and flash overlay (1981)

Flower with encased double overlay (1980)

Fancy-cut crystal-encased bouquet (1989)

Bouquet with double overlay (1989)

Bird picture cane in an encased double overlay (1978)

Butterfly with encased double overlay (early 1980s)

Skier and holly on lace (1977)

Identification

The process of identification answers the following two questions:

Was the weight made by Perthshire?

If it was, which weight is it?

Some of the steps used to answer the first question are the same as those used to answer the second. The simple, four-step process below, when used with the information in the remainder of this chapter, should lead to the answer to both questions.

1. Look for a date or signature.

2. Note all of the physical characteristics.

3. Carefully analyze the design and cane group patterns.

4. Look through the appropriate sections of the book to find a pattern/design match.

Using this process should result in positive identification of more than 95 percent of all Perthshire weights, even the one-of-a-kind pieces.

Signatures and Dates

Was it made by Perthshire? Perhaps the easiest way to answer this question is to look for a signature or signature/date cane. If you don't find one, other characteristics of the weight must be examined closely.

Nearly all Perthshire paperweights contain either a cane with the letter "P" in it, or, alternatively, a cane with a "P" that includes a date. In a few cases, Perthshire used a "PP" with the date. The numbers making up the date are in individual canes in some early weights.

The signature cane is often found in the center of the design or on the underside of the weight. However, it may be incorporated into the design, perhaps in the outer ring of canes or even hidden somewhere in the setup, such as in the middle of a flower. This is especially true when the ground is clear. Occasionally the signature is not a cane, but just the letter "P" scratched into the bottom surface or on the side near the bottom of the weight.

Scratch-signed "P"

Examples of "P" canes with dates

Examples of "P" canes

CAUTION: The "P" signature has been used by other paperweight makers. Pairpoint and Johne Parsley are but two of the possible signatures that may be confused with the Perthshire "P."

On rare occasions, Perthshire weights bear not only the factory signature, but also that of the artist. Examples include:

The 1970B Flash Overlay which has "AM" (for Anton Moravec) and "JA" (for Jack Allan), as well as "1970" and "P" scratched into the base.

The 1971C Crown which has a "JA" cane (for Jack Allan) in the base and no Perthshire signature.

Some 1978E weights with a "JD" cane (for John Deacons) in the base in addition to a "P" in the center of the design.

Magnum millefiori weights that contain a "PM^{C}D" cane (for Peter McDougall) in the setup in addition to a dated "P" cane.

The piedouche made by Peter Mc-Dougall of Perthshire in collaboration with Johne Parsley, which has a cane with the letters "PM" and "JP" arranged so that a "PP" signature is formed as well.

Perthshire sometimes scratched the certificate number into the base of the weight in addition to dating it. A few weights have a certificate number and no other identification.

Some Perthshire weights have a letter other than "P" in the center of the weight. These other letters occur in only a few specific designs, and the letter can be used not only to identify the weight, but also to date it. PP14 and PP32 are weights that have letters signifying dates. The PP14 is the only weight that was made with each letter of the alphabet from "A" (1969) through "Z" (1994).

At the end of this chapter, there is a multipage chart showing the production years for Limited Edition and General Range weights and the years in which design changes occurred. This chart can be used to limit the range of possibilities if you have a dated weight.

1969	A
1970	B
1971	C
1972	D
1973	E
1974	F
1975	G
1976	H
1977	I
1978	J
1979	K
1980	L
1981	M
1982	N
1983	O
1984	P
1985	Q
1986	R
1987	S
1988	T
1989	U
1990	V
1991	W
1992	X
1993	Y
1994	Z

Perthshire letter designations for years

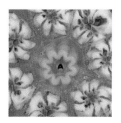

"A" cane used in the 1969 PP14 (first year of issue)

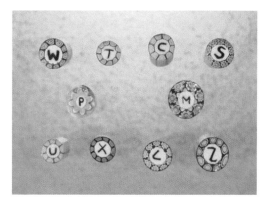

Perthshire letter canes

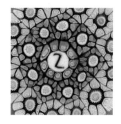

"Z" cane used in the 1994 PP14 (last year of issue)

Characteristics and Style

If the weight has no signature or date, the next step is to determine if it looks like a Perthshire. With the millefiori weights, this is not as difficult as it sounds. As you page through this book, you will see the style and "feel" of the Perthshire canes and layouts.

Canes and Twists. Unlike the canes in antique weights, specific cane characteristics such as the number of cogs are not specific to the factory. However, Perthshire canes have several characteristics that contribute to the Perthshire style.

Perthshire is known for its complex canes made by bundling many simple canes together. Whether simple or complex, Perthshire canes are typically very well formed. Even the most complex canes are extremely precise. Most weights also include twist canes or strips of latticinio. These often extend from the center to the outer edge, i.e., radially, and divide groups of canes into segments with a specific pattern. Many weight designs use simple eight-pointed star canes to outline or fill in pattern areas.

While most of the simple canes exhibit common characteristics, the complex canes are of almost limitless patterns. For example, no two canes in the 1989G Closepack are alike.

PP178

1989G

Examples of weights with simple (PP178) and complex (1989G) Perthshire canes

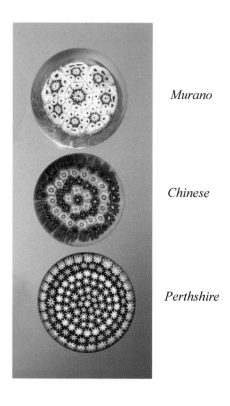

Murano

Chinese

Perthshire

Comparison of typical Murano and Chinese weights with a simple Perthshire

Beginning collectors sometimes find Murano or Chinese millefiori weights and assume that, because they are millefiori, they might be Perthshire. However, once a comparison is made between the types of canes, the collector is quick to recognize that there is really no comparison as far as the quality, detail, size, and color of the canes.

162

Perthshire incorporates picture canes, either black and white or colored, and also silhouette canes into many of its designs. Silhouettes are shapes filled in with a single color (either molded or made by stacking rods), while picture canes are made by stacking many rods of various colors to make a full-color or black and white picture. When examined with a magnifying glass, the edge irregularities from the glass rods are visible. You can quickly learn to recognize many of these canes as being uniquely Perthshire. These specialty canes offer an opportunity to develop an interesting subcollection.

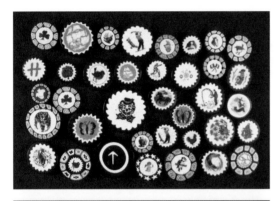

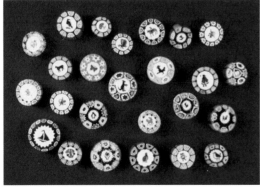

Examples of Perthshire's picture canes

Grounds. Quite often the canes and twists are placed on a color ground, either opaque or translucent. With very few exceptions, Limited Edition weights have a ground of lace or translucent color. General Range weights often have an opaque ground.

PP1, PP2, and PP3 General Range weights made during the first few years that the factory was in operation sometimes have grounds in pastel colors that set them apart from weights made in later years. Many collectors treasure these weights for their exceptional colors and because they are among the first Perthshire weights.

Bases. The bases of most early Perthshire weights are either fire-polished or ground flat and polished. The flat bases of early PP4, PP5, PP6 and PP10 weights were star-cut. After approximately 1974, most Perthshire weights were made with a hollow-ground base. Pictures of the various bases and cuttings are shown on the following page.

Weights with Flat Bases

1977A	
PP4	1969 through 1971
PP5	1969 through 1971
PP6	1969 through 1971
PP9	
PP10	
PP11	1969 through 1974
PP12	1969 through 1974
PP13	1970 through 1974
PP14	
PP20	
PP21	some
PP77	

Some Typical Bottom Cuts and Finishes Used By Perthshire

Grid cut
1990B

Diamond cut
1987D

Strawberry cut
1986D

Feather cut
1994F

Simple star cut
PP10

Star cut with flat surfaces
between the rays
1985B

"V" groove star cut
1979G

Star cut with wide flat
areas between the rays
1992F

Long star cut
1970B

Star cut with different
length rays
PP14

Hollow-ground base

Fire-polished base

The Perthshire Style. The only way to get a sense of the Perthshire style and "feel" is to look at a large number of Perthshire weights or the pictures in this book until the commonality forms an image in your memory. This will also help you to recognize the picture and silhouette canes that Perthshire has used. But remember, new canes are designed every year.

Lampwork weights and weights with a combination of lampwork and millefiori do not exhibit this "feel" as much, but, fortunately, almost all Perthshire lampwork or combination millefiori/lampwork weights are signed.

Which Perthshire Weight Is It?

One approach would be to page through this book until you find a match, but remember that colors vary in many Perthshire Limited Edition and General Range weights and in a few Annual Collection weights, even though the design remains the same. Some combinations of colors, particularly in millefiori designs, can make the appearance so different that misidentification, or even no identification, occurs. There is a better way.

Weights with Signatures and Dates. The task is greatly simplified if you find a signature with a date. You can then proceed to the various sections of the Catalogue and find the range of weights made in that year. In the case of Limited Edition and General Range weights, the easiest way to identify the possible PP numbers is to use the chart at the end of this chapter, which shows production years for all designs with PP numbers.

Next, look at the characteristics of the weight. It will have a combination of physical characteristics that will quickly identify it. Important characteristics to look for are listed on the next page.

Note that the only thing that differentiates PP12s from PP13s is a correlation between ground or lace colors and production years. Through 1975, all of these weights were made with a translucent color under a white lace ground, with the PP12 color differing from the PP13 color each year. All subsequent weights have a colored lace ground with the lace colors being different for PP12s and PP13s each year. Therefore, only by noting the date and the color combination and referring to the chart below, can it be determined whether the weight is a PP12 or a PP13.

Signed Weights with No Date. If you find a signature, but no date, especially in a millefiori weight, you probably have a "PP Something" weight. Use the physical characteristics listed on the next page to determine what type of weight you have. *Size is very important.* Next, study the design. What is unique about it?

	1969	1970	1971	1972	1973	1974	1975	1976	1977
PP12	Blue	Green	Light Green	Blue	Blue	Blue	Indigo	Blue	Blue
PP13		Blue	Amethyst	Amethyst	Amethyst		Honey Amber	Pink	Orange
	White lace ground over color							Colored Lace	

Chart of PP12 and PP13 colors by years

Characteristics Important for Identification

Type
    Millefiori
    Lampwork
    Millefiori/lampwork combined

Millefiori   *Lampwork*   *Combination*
(PP175)   *(1996G)*   *(1983E)*

Size (diameter at the widest point)
    Sizes are approximate
    Small: 2 inches or less
    Medium: 2-1/2 inches
    Large: 3 inches
    Magnum: over 3-1/2 inches

Shape
    Domed
    Faceted
    Fluted (pressed)
    Pedestal (piedouche)
    Other (knobs, bottles, dishes, etc.)

Domed   *Faceted*   *Fluted*
(1997G)   *(1986G)*   *(PP53)*

Bases (photos on page 164)
    Flat and polished
    Fire-polished
    Hollow-ground
    Cutting type

Pedestal
(1990G)

Special Designs
    Christmas
    Commemoratives
    Souvenirs

Design Features
    Hollow
    Ground type (lace, latticinio, clear, translucent color or opaque color)
    Overlays (translucent flash or opaque single, double, or triple)

Pattern or design of the setup
    Number and arrangement of flowers, canes, etc.
    Special canes
    Crowns

Color
    Setups
    Grounds
    Bases
    Overlays

Look carefully at the layout. Are there twist canes that separate the millefiori canes into pie-shaped segments? Do the twists, if any, only radiate out from the center, or are they laid out in a pattern or a ring around the center?

Next look closely at the pattern of the millefiori cane groups. Counting out from the center, decide what specific pattern you see. Are the canes between the radials in a 1-1-2-3, a 1-2-3-3, or some other pattern? See the example shown on page 76 in the Catalogue for help in describing patterns.

Now, armed with the specifics of the weight, go through the book until you find a specific match. Remember that colors vary and can be deceiving. Colors are not specific to a given design unless they are stated in the description.

Cautions and Caveats

Differences in colors and faceting, while sometimes helpful, can be misleading.

Colors, both of the ground and of the millefiori or lampwork, are often not specific as to design. A pattern may stand out much more in some combinations of colors than it does in other color combinations.

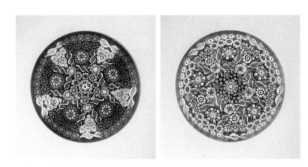

PP169 weights in different color combinations

PP142, domed   PP142A, faceted

Faceting can alter the appearance of a weight dramatically. Some weights were issued in both faceted and domed versions. For example, the PP142 is domed and the PP142A is the identical pattern, but faceted. When color and faceting variations are combined, a dramatic difference in appearance can result. It is therefore neccessary to look closely to identify patterns.

PP1 faceted after leaving the factory

Facets may have been added to some weights at a later date by someone other than Perthshire. Perhaps this was done to repair some damage, or maybe someone just thought it would be interesting to facet it.

A strange or unidentifiable pattern, while possibly an indication of a somewhat unique weight, may be just a variation of a regular pattern. The factory setup teams have been known to add an extra

167

twist or a few extra canes on occasion. These minor variations within a design concept are usually called design variations and have no affect as to either the collectibility or value of the piece. Only the Limited Edition weights and the Annual Collection weights are absolutely (almost) true to the design. General Range weights do, although not often, vary slightly from the standard designs. See the PP1 weights in the Catalogue for examples of pattern variation.

The PP5 (domed or with top facet and six side facets) and PP60 (top facet only) are defined as "an assortment of designs set on a translucent color ground, with a 2-1/2 inch diameter." Since these designs can vary, quite often a millefiori weight which fits no other specific design, but is the right size and has a color ground, turns out to be one of these.

In summary

1. Look for a date or signature.

2. Note size and all of the other physical characteristics.

3. Carefully analyze the design and cane group patterns.

4. Look through the appropriate sections of the Catalogue to find a pattern/design match.

Steps 1 to 3 will let you quickly eliminate all of the weights which do not fit as to size, date, significant features or canes, etc., and will lead you to the proper parts of the Catalogue to facilitate quick identification.

Weight Identification Examples

Example 1: You have a large (3-inch diameter) weight with an opaque turquoise color ground, a center butterfly picture cane surrounded by a ring of canes, ten radial twists (radiating from the center), that separate cane groups of 1-1-2-3, then a ring of twists and an outer ring of canes, and a "P" cane in the base (underside).

Using these specific details, you can easily determine that you have a PP109, even though the ground of the PP109 pictured in the Catalogue happens to be blue. The design pattern is specific.

Example 2: You have a medium-sized (2-1/2 inch diameter) weight with a translucent blue color ground, four short twists radiating from a center cane and separating cane groups of 1-3, then a ring

of canes and two outer rings of canes, each having sixteen canes separated by short radial twists that cross both rings, and a "1987" date cane. By going to the chart of production years for Limited Edition and General Range weights and finding the range of PP numbers for weights made in 1987, you find that the description of the PP99 design fits exactly, even though, because of the colors, the shapes of the canes, and the size of the center radial twists, the weight has an appearance quite different from the one in the book.

Example 3: You have a large (3-1/8 inch) weight with a bouquet of three small purple flowers, a flower with six brown petals with white stripes, and a pink, multipetaled flower with a white center on a clear ground. The weight has a top facet and two rows of eight side facets each, a star-cut base, and a "P" cane in the setup near the bouquet.

Looking in the Annual Collection category (since this is a lampwork weight), it is necessary to browse through the pictures since the weight is undated. Observation shows a similarity to the picture of the 1979G weight pictured and the description confirms that the flower colors and types vary in this design.

Example 4: You have a large (3-1/8 inch) weight with a translucent green ground, center orange flower with three buds and green leaves, six touching millefiori circlets forming a garland that is purple in the center and half green, half orange on the outside, and a "P1983" cane in the base.

In looking at the Annual Collection weights from 1983, it is obvious that this is not one of them. The pattern is somewhat similar to that of the "C" weight from the 1982 Annual Collection, but the center flower, ground color, and date cane do not fit the description and the garland is also different. Also, you can tell it is not a Limited Edition weight from 1983, by looking at weights that fit that category. Therefore—you have a one-of-a-kind!

Happy Hunting!

Limited Edition and General Range Production Years

	1969	1970	1971	1972	1973	1974	1975	1976	1977	1978	1979	1980	1981	1982	1983	1984	1985	1986	1987	1988	1989	1990	1991	1992	1993	1994	1995	1996	1997
PP1	x	x	x	x	x	x	x	x	x	c	x	x	x	c	x	c	x	x	x	x	x	x	x	x	x	x	x	x	x
PP2	x	x	x	x	x	x	x	x	x	c	x	x	x	x	x	x	x	x	x	x	x	x	x	x	x	x	x	x	x
PP2A																													
PP3	x	x	x	x	x	x	x	x								c	x	x	x	x	x	x	x	x	x	x	x	x	x
PP4	x	x	x	c	x	x	x	x	x	x	x	x	x	x	x	x	x	x	x	x	x	x	x	x	c	x	x	c	x
PP5	x	x	x	c	x	x	x	x	x	x	x	x	x	x	x	x	x	x	x	x	x	x	x	x	x	x	x	c	x
PP6	x	x	x	c	x	x	x	x	x																				
PP7	x	x	x																										
PP8	x	x	x																										
PP9	x	x	x	x	x	x	x	x	x	x	x	x																	
PP10	x	x	x	x	x	x	x	x	x	x	x	x	x	x	x	x	x	x	x	x	x	x							
PP11	x	x	x	c	x	x	x	x	x	x	x	x	x	x	c	x	x	x	x	x	x	x	c	c					
PP12	x	x	x	x	x	x	x	c	x																				
PP13				x	x	x	x	c	x																				
PP14	x	x	x	x	x	x	x	x	x	x	x	x	x	x	x	x	x	x	x	x	x	x	x	x	x	c			
PP15	x	x	x	x	x	x	x	x	x	x	x	x	x	x	x	x	x	x	x	x	x	x	x	x	x	x			
PP16	x	x																											
PP17	x	x	x	x	x	x	x	x	x	x						x	x	x	x	x	x	x	x	c	x	x	x	x	x
PP18	x	x	x	x	x	x				x												x	x	c	x	x	x	x	x
PP18A																											x	x	x
PP18B																													
PP18C																													
PP19	x	x	x	x	x	x	x	x	x	x	x	x					x	x	x	x	x	x	x	c	x	x	x	x	x
PP19A																									x	x	x	x	x
PP20			x	x	x	c	x	x																					
PP21			x						x																				
PP22					x	x	x	x	x	x	x	x	x	x	c	x	x	x	x	x	x	x	x	x	x	x	x	x	
PP23					x	x	x																						
PP24				x																									
PP25						x	x																						
PP26						x	x																						
PP27							x																						
PP28								x	x	c	x	x	x	x	c	x	x	x	x	x	x	x	x						
PP29							x																						
PP30							x	x	x	x	x	x																	
PP31										x	c	c	c	c	c	c													
PP32										x	c	c	c	c	c	c	c	c											
PP33										x	x																		
PP34										x	x																		
PP35										x	x	x																	
PP36											x																		
PP37											x																		
PP38												x																	
PP39												x																	
PP40												x																	
PP41												x	x	x															
PP42												x	x	x	x	x	x	x	c	x	x	c	x	c	x	x			
PP43												x	x	x	x	x	x	x	c	x	x	x	x	x	x	x			
PP44													x																
PP45													x																

Note: **x** indicates weight made that year; **c** indicates a design change that year

Limited Edition and General Range Production Years

	1969	1970	1971	1972	1973	1974	1975	1976	1977	1978	1979	1980	1981	1982	1983	1984	1985	1986	1987	1988	1989	1990	1991	1992	1993	1994	1995	1996	1997
PP46													x	x	x	x	x	c	x	x	x	c	x	x	c	x	x	c	c
PP47													x	x	x	x	x	x	x	x	x	c	c	x	c	c	c	c	c
PP48													x	x		x			x	x	x	x	x	x	x	x			
PP49														x															
PP50														x															
PP51	not issued																												
PP52															x	x	x	x	x	x	x	x	x	x	x	x	x	x	x
PP53														x	x	x	x	x	x	x	x	x	x	x	x	x	x	x	x
PP54															x														
PP55	not issued																												
PP56																	x	x	x	x	x	x	x	x	x	x	x	c	c
PP57															x	x													
PP58															x	x	x	x	x	x	x	x	x	x	x	x	x	x	c
PP59														x	x	x	x	x	x	x	x	x	x	x	x	x	x	x	x
PP60															x	x	x	x	x	x	x	x	x	x	x	x	x		
PP61															x	x	x	c	x	x	x	x	x	x	x	c	x	x	x
PP62															x	x	x	x	x	x	x	x	x	x	x	x	x	c	
PP63																c	c	c	c	c	c	c	c	c	c	c	c	c	
PP64															x														
PP65															x	x	x												
PP66															x	x	x												
PP67															x	x	x	x											
PP68															x	x	x												
PP69															x	x	x												
PP70																x	x												
PP71																x													
PP72																x													
PP73																x	x	x	x	x	x	x	x	x	x	x	x	x	x
PP74																x	x												
PP75																	x	x	x	x	x	x	x	x	x	x	x	x	x
PP76																	x	x	x	x	x	x	x	x	x	x	x	x	x
PP77																	x	x											
PP78																	x	x											
PP79																	x												
PP80																	x	x	x	x	x	x	c	c	c	c	c	c	
PP81																	x	x	x	x	x	x	x	x	x	x	c		
PP82																	x	x	x	x	x	x							
PP83																	x	x	x	x	x	x	x	x	c	x	x	x	x
PP84																		x	x	x									
PP85																		x	x	x									
PP86																		x	x	x									
PP87																			x	x	x	x	x	x	x	x	c	c	
PP88																			x	x	x	x	x	x	x	x	c	x	x
PP89																			x	x	x	x							
PP90																			x	x									
PP91																			x	x	x	x	x	x					
PP92																						x	x	x	x				
PP93																			x	x	x	x	x	x	c	x	x	x	x
PP94																						x	x	x	c	x	x	x	x
PP95																			x										

Note: **x** indicates weight made that year; **c** indicates a design change that year

171

Limited Edition and General Range Production Years

	1969	1970	1971	1972	1973	1974	1975	1976	1977	1978	1979	1980	1981	1982	1983	1984	1985	1986	1987	1988	1989	1990	1991	1992	1993	1994	1995	1996	1997
PP96																			x										
PP97																			x										
PP98																			x										
PP99																			x										
PP100																				x									
PP101																			x	x									
PP102																			x	x									
PP103																			x	x									
PP104																			x	x									
PP105																			x	x									
PP106																				x									
PP107																					x	x	x	x	x	x	x	x	
PP108																					x	x	x	x	x	x	x	x	x
PP109																					x	x	x	x	x	x	x	x	x
PP110																				x	x								
PP111																					x								
PP112																					x								
PP113																					x								
PP114																					x								
PP115																					x	x							
PP116																					x								
PP117																					x								
PP118																					x								
PP119																					x	x	c	x	x	x	x	x	x
PP120																					x	x							
PP121																					x								
PP122																						x	x	x	x	x	x		
PP123																						x	x	x	x	x	x	x	x
PP124																						x	x	x	x	x	x	c	x
PP125																						x							
PP126																						x							
PP127																						x							
PP128																						x							
PP129																						x							
PP130																						x							
PP131																						x							
PP132																						x	x	x	x	x			
PP133																						x	x	x	x				
PP133A																											x		
PP134																							x	x	x	x			
PP135																							x						
PP136																							x						
PP137																							x						
PP138																							x						
PP139																							x						
PP140																							x						
PP141																								x					
PP142																								x					
PP143																								x					
PP144																								x					

172

Note: **x** indicates weight made that year; **c** indicates a design change that year

Limited Edition and General Range Production Years

	1969	1970	1971	1972	1973	1974	1975	1976	1977	1978	1979	1980	1981	1982	1983	1984	1985	1986	1987	1988	1989	1990	1991	1992	1993	1994	1995	1996	1997
PP145																								x					
PP146																								x					
PP147																								x					
PP148																								x					
PP149																									x				
PP150																									x				
PP151																									x				
PP152																									x				
PP153																									x				
PP154																									x				
PP155																									x				
PP156																										x	x	x	x
PP156A																											x	x	c
PP157																										x			
PP158																										x	x		
PP159																										x			
PP160																										x			
PP161																										x			
PP162																										x			
PP163																											x	x	x
PP164																											x		
PP165																											x		
PP166																											x		
PP167																											x		
PP168																											x		
PP169																											x		
PP170																												x	x
PP171																												x	x
PP172																												x	
PP173																												x	x
PP174																												x	x
PP175																												x	x
PP176																												x	x
PP177																												x	
PP178																													x
PP178A																													x
PP179																													x
PP180																													x
PP181																													x
PP182																													x
PP183																													x
PP184																													x
PP185																													x

Note: **x** indicates weight made that year; **c** indicates a design change that year

Glossary

(Refer to the Catalogue for cited examples.)

ANNEAL. To lower the temperature of a newly formed weight by placing it in an oven which is cooled slowly over many hours. (At Perthshire this is about 24 hours.) This reduces the internal stress in the glass which could cause the weight to crack at some later time.

ANNEALING OVEN. See ANNEAL. The oven into which hot weights are placed to allow them to cool slowly. See pages 12 and 13.

ANNUAL COLLECTION WEIGHTS. Specially designed weights, typically of lampwork, complex millefiori patterns, or a combination, that were made in limited quantities during a specific year. Example: 1969A.

BARBER POLE. A weight in which the individual canes are separated by white latticinio rods containing one or more colored threads. See also CHECKER. Example: 1993C.

BASAL RIM. The outer ring of the bottom of a weight with a concave base. The BASAL RIM contacts the surface on which the weight rests.

BASE. The underside of a weight. The bottom of the weight.

BASKET. A cup or bowl shape made (typically) of staves or latticinio strips, above or into which the primary design element is placed. Example: 1988A.

BATCH. The term used to describe the mixture of sand and other ingredients to be melted to make glass.

BEEHIVE FACETING. See HONEY-COMB FACETING.

BOUQUET. A group of flowers placed together to form the setup. It may be flat or three-dimensional. Examples: flat - 1991F; three-dimensional - 1991G.

CANE. A single rod of glass containing a pattern that is visible from the side (TWIST CANE) or in cross-section (MILLEFIORI CANE). **Also:** A short slice or piece from either a millefiori cane or a twist cane used as one of the elements in a millefiori design. As used in the Catalogue Chapter of this book, the word CANE refers to a slice of millefiori cane used as an element in the SETUP or design. The term TWIST is used to refer to twist canes.

CANE CLUSTER. A small group of millefiori canes, typically used as part of a design. Example: 1982C.

CARPET GROUND. A ground made by placing many identical millefiori canes close together. Example: 1994B.

CHECKER (CHEQUER). A pattern where the individual millefiori canes are separated by strips of colored glass or white latticinio canes. Examples: colored strips - 1991C; white latticinio strips - PP11 (1990).

CHESSBOARD. A pattern of adjacent squares. Example: PP35.

CIRCLET. A small ring or circle of millefiori canes. Example: 1975C.

CLEAR GROUND. A gather of clear (uncolored) glass used as a ground. When viewed, the setup appears to be floating in the clear glass. See also OPAQUE, TRANSPARENT and TRANSLUCENT. Example: 1995E.

CLOSE CONCENTRIC. A pattern of concentric rings of canes, each ring touching or nearly touching the adjacent rings. See also CONCENTRIC and OPEN CONCENTRIC. Example: PP4.

CLOSE MILLEFIORI. Millefiori canes placed very close together so as to touch or nearly touch. The term can apply to an area of a weight or to a ring of canes. See also CLOSEPACK. Example: 1989G.

CLOSEPACK (CLOSEPACKED). Many millefiori canes placed so as to touch or nearly touch, completely covering a part of or the entire design area of the weight. See also CLOSE MILLEFIORI.

CLUSTER. A group of canes placed close together to form a single design element. Example: 1993D.

COG CANE. A cane with "teeth" or ridges around the perimeter.

COLORED PICTURE CANE. See PICTURE CANE.

COLOR GROUND. A layer of colored glass used to form the ground. May be OPAQUE, TRANSLUCENT or TRANSPARENT. Sometimes has a mottled appearance if colored chips are fused together.

COMPLEX MILLEFIORI CANE. A cane made by combining several simple canes or groups of canes and then fusing them together to form a complex pattern within a single cane.

CONCENTRIC. A pattern made from circles of canes, one within the next, all having a common center point. Example: PP4.

CRIMP. A tool made from metal and shaped to form a rose or other design form when it is pressed into the hot glass.

CRIMP WEIGHT. A weight containing a design made using a CRIMP. Example: PP133A.

CROWN. The upper part of the weight. The gather of glass placed above the setup. See also DOME.

CROWN WEIGHT. A weight with ribbons or latticinio rods running from the top center outward and down the sides to the bottom. Example: 1969A.

CUSHION. A ground on which the setup is placed. It is usually somewhat dome-shaped (convex) and can be made of spiral latticinio or colored glass. Examples: latticinio cushion - 1984D; colored glass cushion - 1989E.

CUTTING. The finishing of the outside of a weight by grinding facets or decorative designs into the surface. A star-cut pattern on the bottom of a weight is one type of cutting. Example: 1982H.

DATE CANE. A cane with a date in it referring to the year of production or the date of an event being commemorated. It can be a single cane, or individual canes for each numeral fused together. See page 159.

DESIGN. The overall layout or pattern of the weight, including the interior elements and the surface cutting. See also MAIN DESIGN ELEMENT.

DIAMETER. The widest measurement across the horizontal direction of the weight. This is the most common measurement used to determine the size of a weight.

DIAMOND CUT. Two sets of parallel cuts on the base of the weight that cross at an angle of other than 90 degrees to form many small diamond shapes. See also GRID CUT, FEATHER CUT, and STRAWBERRY CUT. See page 164.

DIMENSIONAL BOUQUET. A flower bouquet where each flower is formed in three dimensions. See also FLAT BOUQUET. Example: 1993G.

DOME. Convex surface of the upper part (the CROWN) of the weight. The curvature of the DOME magnifies the setup.

DOMED WEIGHT. A weight with an upper surface that is smoothly curved like a sphere or a ball and is not faceted. Example: 1991E.

DOUBLE (OR TRIPLE) OVERLAY. See OVERLAY WEIGHT.

DOUBLE SPIRAL LATTICINIO. See LATTICINIO.

DOUBLE SWIRL LATTICINIO. See LATTICINIO.

ENCASE. To surround the setup with molten glass, thereby forming a paperweight.

ENCASED OVERLAY. A weight with a layer of clear glass completely surrounding a smaller overlaid weight within. The inner weight and the outer layer of clear glass are usually cut with fancy patterns. See the Special Editions section in this book.

END-OF-DAY WEIGHT. So named from the practice of taking whatever canes and pieces that were left over at the end of the day and combining them all into a random-patterned weight. See also: SCRAMBLED WEIGHT. Example: PP19.

END-OF-WEEK WEIGHT (BOTTLE). See END-OF-DAY WEIGHT. Perthshire shows END-OF-DAY weights (PP19) and END-OF-WEEK bottles. Example: PP52.

FACET. A flat or concave window cut into the surface of the weight, thereby changing the magnification of the setup when viewed through the faceted area. Typical faceting is one large top facet, and five or six side facets. More than one row of side facets can be used. Sometimes called a PRINTY.

FEATHER CUT. A combination of a GRID or DIAMOND CUT and a STAR CUT. This results in a bottom design where the raised areas between the rays of the star have a GRID or DIAMOND pattern, giving the appearance of a feather. See page 164.

FINGER CUT (FINGER FACETS). See FLUTE.

FIRE POLISH. To use a torch or flame to melt a glass surface thereby smoothing it. FIRE POLISHING is often used to smooth the sharp edges of the PONTIL MARK after the weight is broken off the PONTIL ROD. See page 164.

FLASH. A layer of non-OPAQUE colored glass placed on the surface or base of a weight. It is often used as an overlay and then partly cut away by faceting. Examples: flash overlay - 1992E; flash base - 1993G.

FLAT BOUQUET. A group of two-dimensional flowers placed together to form the main design element. See also NOSEGAY and DIMENSIONAL BOUQUET. Example: 1994E.

FLOATING DESIGN. A design placed well above the ground or basket. Example: 1986 Christmas weight.

FLORET. A slice of millefiori cane. See CANE. **Also:** A small CLUSTER of millefiori canes used to represent a flower or flowers. Example: 1993B.

FLOWER WEIGHT. A weight which has a single large flower as the main design feature. Example: 1983A.

FLUTE. A deep, elongated cut placed vertically on the side of a weight. See also FINGER CUT . Example: 1985D.

FOOT. A wide, flat piece attached to and extending out from the base of a weight or a pedestal stem. Example: PP133.

FURNACE. A gas or electric heating unit containing the POT where the BATCH is melted to make glass.

GARLAND. A ring of canes or small lampworked pieces that surrounds and accents the MAIN DESIGN ELEMENT. The ring can also be shaped to form lobes or loops. The GARLAND itself can be the MAIN DESIGN ELEMENT. Two or more lobed (looped) garlands can be intertwined to form a complex garland. Example: 1980G.

GATHER. A quantity of molten glass obtained by dipping the PONTIL ROD into the POT containing the glass. The GATHER is used to pick up or encase the setup, to fill MOLDS to make millefiori CANES, or for a variety of other uses, such as to make the base of a weight or parts of other glass pieces, e.g., the handle on the Cream Pitcher (PP23). It can also be rolled in powdered colored glass and then rolled or shaped on a steel plate to make colored glass.

GENERAL RANGE WEIGHT. A weight which is issued in unlimited quantities, usually over several years. Examples: PP1, PP2, PP3.

GEOMETRIC FACETING. Many small facets all over the surface of the weight. Somewhat similar to HONEYCOMB FACETING, but usually not as extensive. Example: 1994G.

GLASS TRANSFER. A decal which is fired onto a glass disk which is then encased.

GRID CUT. Two sets of many parallel cuts set at 90 degree angles to make many small squares. See also DIAMOND CUT, FEATHER CUT, and STRAWBERRY CUT. See page 164.

GROUND. The layer of glass on which the main design rests. Some types of GROUNDS are MOSS, CARPET, LACE, LATTICINIO, COLOR, and CLEAR.

HOLLOW-GROUND BASE. The bottom of a weight where the PONTIL MARK has been ground away leaving a concave bottom with a BASAL RIM around the perimeter. See page 164.

HOLLOW WEIGHT. A weight which has a hollow interior within which the main design element (usually a three dimensional lampwork animal) is placed. Example: 1983G.

HONEYCOMB CANE. A cane that has a honeycomb appearance. Example: 1988B.

HONEYCOMB FACETING. All-over small facets that cause the internal design to appear many times at the surface of the weight. Also called BEEHIVE FACETING. See also GEOMETRIC FACETING. Example: 1989F.

INK BOTTLE. A bottle containing a millefiori or lampwork design in the bottom and in the stopper. Example: PP83.

INK WELL. Same as INK BOTTLE.

INTERTWINED GARLANDS. Two or more GARLANDS interlaced to form a complex pattern. An INTERTWINED trefoil GARLAND results in a pattern with six lobes—three from each trefoil. Each GARLAND is continuous and usually of a single type of cane. See also LOOPED GARLAND. Example: 1978E.

LACE GROUND. A ground made of jumbled latticinio pieces to give an appearance of lace. Also known as UPSET MUSLIN. Example: 1993E.

LAMP. A burner or torch that uses gas and oxygen. Lampworkers use this burner to melt or soften small pieces of glass so that they can be hand-formed into flowers, animals, etc.

LAMPWORK (LAMPWORKED). A design element made by forming the individual parts over a LAMP and then joining them together to form the finished motif. See page 10.

LARGE WEIGHT. A weight with a diameter of about 3 inches. See also MAGNUM.

LATTICINIO. Clear glass rods containing white or other solid colored glass threads which have been twisted during the PULL. **Also:** A GROUND of spiraled white or colored glass threads. It can be shaped as a CUSHION (convex), a BASKET (concave), or flat. A **Single** Spiral Latticinio twists in only one direction. When a **Single** Spiral Latticinio ground is viewed from the top or bottom, the glass threads sometimes may appear to cross, but when viewed from the side it is obvious that they do not. When they appear to cross, it is sometimes referred to as "Double Swirl" Latticinio. A **Double** Spiral Latticinio has a second set of threads that twist in the opposite direction from the first set. This is obvious by noting that the threads cross when viewed from the side. **Double** Spiral Latticinio appears to be made only by Perthshire. Examples: Single Spiral - 1993B; Double Swirl - 1976A; Double Spiral - 1973B.

LATTICINIO BASKET. A basket-shaped (concave) GROUND made from spiral latticinio. The term LATTICINIO BASKET is sometimes used to refer to any latticinio GROUND, regardless of shape. Example: 1994C.

LIMITED EDITION WEIGHT. Weight made in a quantity of not more than a preset limit during one or more years. Perthshire categorizes some of the weights within their "PP" numbering system as LIMITED EDITIONS to differentiate from other weights made in unlimited quantities. All of the ANNUAL COLLECTION WEIGHTS are also produced in specified limited quantities (but only for one year) and are therefore also LIMITED EDITIONS, but are not part of the LIMITED EDITION category. See also GENERAL RANGE WEIGHT. Example: PP81.

LOOPED GARLAND. One or more garlands which are shaped to form loops or lobes. Example: 1980G.

MAGNUM. A weight with a diameter of more than 3 inches.

MAIN DESIGN ELEMENT. The lampwork motif or millefiori design that is the primary design of the paperweight.

MEDIUM (SIZED) WEIGHT. A weight approximately 2-1/2 inches in diameter.

MILLEFIORI. From the Italian words for "Thousand Flowers." A glass rod formed from various colors of glass, such that its cross-section resembles a flower.

MILLEFIORI CANE. See CANE.

MINIATURE WEIGHT. Weight with a diameter of less than 2 inches. Note that with regard to the ANNUAL COLLECTION WEIGHTS, Perthshire refers to MINIATURE WEIGHTS to indicate that they are of a small size compared to full-sized weights. ANNUAL COLLECTION WEIGHTS called "Miniature" can be over 2 inches in diameter.

MOLD. A metal shape into which molten glass is pressed to form canes. See pages 8 and 13.

MOSS GROUND. A ground of green canes with many individual rods within each cane to give a moss-like appearance. Example: 1976E.

MOTIF. The main design of a weight.

MUSHROOM. An encased group of millefiori canes, usually of closepack or concentric pattern, which has long canes at the perimeter. These long canes are pulled down and to the center to form a stem. When viewed from the side the design has a mushroom shape. Example: 1986F.

MUSLIN GROUND. Same as LACE ground. Also sometimes called UPSET MUSLIN.

NEWEL POST. Large weight mounted on a metal (usually) base intended to be attached to a post on a staircase. See Special Editions in the Catalogue Chapter.

NOSEGAY. A FLAT BOUQUET in which millefiori canes are used as "Flowers." Small lampwork bouquets are also sometimes referred to as NOSEGAYS. Example: 1977A.

ONE-OF-A-KIND. A weight that is unique as to design, cutting, or color. One-of-a-kind weights are created with the intent to make only one weight with that design. PROTOTYPE weights, while quite probably ONE-OF-A-KIND, are created as steps in developing a production design, and the intent in making the PROTOTYPE is to see what it looks like and what changes need to be made to make it producible in quantity.

ONE-OFF. A term sometimes used to refer to a ONE-OF-A-KIND weight.

OPAQUE. Not allowing light to pass through. It is not possible to see through OPAQUE glass. See also TRANSLUCENT and TRANSPARENT. Example: 1974B.

OPEN CONCENTRIC. A concentric pattern where the adjacent concentric rings are spaced from each other and do not touch. Canes within each ring may be close or spaced. See also CONCENTRIC and CLOSE CONCENTRIC. Example: PP61 (1986).

OVERLAY WEIGHT. A weight with one or more layers of colored glass applied to the surface, then partially removed by cutting and faceting. A SINGLE OVERLAY has one layer of colored glass applied to the surface. In this book SINGLE OVERLAY refers to an OPAQUE layer.

A FLASH overlay has a single layer of TRANSLUCENT or TRANSPARENT colored glass applied. A DOUBLE OVERLAY typically has a layer of white glass with a layer of some other color over it. When cut, both the colored and white layers are exposed. A TRIPLE OVERLAY (by far the least common) has a colored layer applied, then a white (usually) layer, and finally another colored layer. When cut, all three layers become visible. See also ENCASED OVERLAY. Examples: Flash Overlay - 1995G; Single Overlay - 1993F; Double Overlay - 1990E; Triple Overlay - 1977C.

PAPER KNIFE. Letter opener. See Paperweight-related Items in the Catalogue Chapter.

PAPERWEIGHT. A glass object, usually somewhat spherical in shape, with a flattened bottom, and having decorations inside which are also usually made entirely from glass.

PATTERN. The design within a weight.

PATTERNED MILLEFIORI WEIGHT. A weight in which millefiori canes, and often twists, are used to create a geometric internal design.

PEDESTAL WEIGHT. Also called a PIE-DOUCHE. A weight placed on top of a column or stem of glass. This stem can be thick or thin, and is often decorated with latticinio strips, a pattern formed into the glass stem, torsades, etc. The pedestal may have a foot. Example: PP133.

PICTURE CANE. A cane where hundreds or even thousands of small rods of glass are stacked and fused together to form a picture. The picture may be black and white or full color. See also SILHOUETTE CANE. Examples: colored picture - 1993 Christmas weight; black and white picture - PP168.

PIEDOUCHE. French term for PEDES-TAL. See PEDESTAL WEIGHT. Example: Perthshire-Parsley Piedouche.

POMPON CANE. A complex millefiori cane made from many curved segments that give an appearance of a many-pet-aled flower. Similar to, but more complex than a Clichy-type rose. Example: PP143.

PONTIL. See PONTIL ROD.

PONTIL MARK. A mark on the bottom of a weight where it was attached to a metal rod (called the PONTIL ROD) while it was being formed.

PONTIL ROD. A hollow metal rod used to gather molten glass from the POT and also to hold the weight while it is being formed. Sometimes referred to as a PUNTY.

POT. A ceramic container inside of the furnace into which the BATCH is placed to be melted into glass. After melting, the POT holds the molten glass in the furnace.

PP. Designation for the GENERAL RANGE and LIMITED EDITION weights made by **P**erthshire **P**aperweights Limited.

PRESSED WEIGHT. A weight which has been pushed into a shaped MOLD while the glass is still soft, resulting in a cog-like or scalloped perimeter. Example: PP53.

PRINTY. See FACET.

PROTOTYPE. A weight produced as a step in creating a design which will become a production weight. PROTO-TYPES, while probably ONE-OF-A-KIND weights, are not created with the intent of making only one weight of that de-sign, but rather as a step leading up to a final, fully developed design for factory production.

PULL. A single length of millefiori cane made by stretching a thick, short rod out to several feet in length while it is hot. This PULL or CANE is then cut into short lengths to be used in making canes of greater complexity or is sliced for use in making millefiori designs.

PUNTY. See FACET. **Also:** Sometimes used to refer to the PONTIL ROD.

RADIAL TWIST. A length of twist cane laid out like a spoke in a wheel. Example: PP108.

RIBBON. A flattened glass rod that usu-ally has a different color on each side with white in between. When twisted, it is often used as an element of a CROWN WEIGHT. In antique usage, latticinio "RIBBONS" are used to make "ribbon crown weights". **Also:** A LAMPWORK piece of colored glass formed into a bow like a hair ribbon. Examples: Flat RIB-BON - 1985 Christmas Crown Weight; RIBBON bow - 1974C.

RING (MILLEFIORI RING). A circle of MILLEFIORI CANES used as part of the MAIN DESIGN ELEMENT. A CONCEN-TRIC design may have several RINGS of canes.

ROD. A piece of long, round, solid-colored glass which can be used to form STAVES or to make part of a millefiori CANE or LAMPWORK design. **Also:** A short length of solid color, twist, or latticinio used as part of the millefiori design.

SCATTERED MILLEFIORI. A weight with individual millefiori canes placed in a loose open pattern or randomly spaced in the weight. Example: PP13 (1975).

SCENT BOTTLE. A small bottle used to hold perfumes. Example: PP22.

SCRAMBLED WEIGHT. A weight made using whole and broken millefiori canes and twists in no set pattern. Example: PP19.

SCRATCH SIGNED. A signature scratched onto the surface of the weight with a diamond pen, usually on or near the bottom. Example: 1977B. See pages 159 and 160.

SETUP. The millefiori design made up of individual canes before they are encased in a weight. **Also:** The LAMPWORKED parts after they are assembled and before they are encased. See pages 10 and 11.

SHOT GLASS. A small drinking glass used to measure quantities of liquors or beverages. **Also:** In antique usage, a weight with a deep cup set on top into which lead shot was placed to hold writing quills. Example: PP43.

SIGNATURE CANE. A CANE containing the initials of the factory (usually "P," but sometimes "PP," for Perthshire) or the individual artist who made the weight. Perthshire signature canes come in several forms, both with and without dates incorporated in them. See page 159.

SILHOUETTE CANE. A CANE containing the filled-in outline of an object or animal, in a solid color that contrasts with the surrounding area of the cane. Some SILHOUETTE CANES are made by casting into a shaped MOLD, while others are made by stacking thin rods and fusing them together. See also PICTURE CANE. Examples: shaped mold - PP148; stacked rods - PP168.

SIMPLE MILLEFIORI CANE. A MILLEFIORI CANE of usually only a few colors and a simple shape. It has never been bundled with other canes to form a complex cane. See also COMPLEX MILLEFIORI CANE. Example: PP178.

SINGLE OVERLAY. See OVERLAY WEIGHT.

SINGLE SPIRAL LATTICINIO. See LATTICINIO.

SMALL WEIGHT. A weight approximately 2 inches in diameter. See also MINIATURE WEIGHT.

SPACED MILLEFIORI. A weight where the individual millefiori canes are separated by some distance. See also CLOSE MILLEFIORI and SCATTERED MILLEFIORI. Example: PP47.

SPECIAL EDITION. A weight made to commemorate some special event, such as the French Revolution, or at the request of a customer such as the Bergstrom-Mahler Museum. **Also:** A very limited series of weights made using very complex and difficult techniques such as DOUBLE OVERLAY ENCASED DOUBLE OVERLAY weights. **Note:** SPECIAL EDITION weights do not appear in the annual catalogues published by Perthshire. The Catalogue Chapter contains a section on Special Edition weights.

SPIRAL LATTICINIO. See LATTICINIO.

SPOKE. A length of millefiori twist or latticinio rod laid out like a spoke in a wheel. See: RADIAL TWIST. Example: PP108.

STAR CUT. A pattern cut into the bottom of a weight to resemble a many-pointed star. The cuts may be of different lengths or different sizes and shapes. See page 164.

STARDUST CANE. A cane made from many small, identical, star-shaped CANES. It is usually white, but can be any other single color.

STAVE. A LATTICINIO or colored glass ROD or CANE placed around the outside of a design and pulled down to form a BASKET or MUSHROOM.

STAVE BASKET. A basket shape made of RODS or CANES into or above which the SETUP is placed. See also LATTICINIO BASKET. Example: 1978F.

STRAWBERRY CUT. A fancy cutting on the bottom of a weight. Three sets of parallel cuts, placed at 120 degree angles, are made to form many small triangles and hexagons. See page 164.

SWIRL CUT. Deep grooves that are cut into the surface of a weight and swirl from the bottom to the top of the weight. May be a clear or an overlaid weight. Example: 1987B.

SWIRL WEIGHT. A weight with flattened rods placed close together, then twisted to form a pinwheel effect. May be used as the main design or as a ground. Example: 1980E.

TORSADE. A ring made from a single TWIST or LATTICINIO ROD joined at the ends to form a continuous piece. It encircles the design and may be placed inside or outside of a weight Example: 1983B.

TRANSLUCENT. Allowing light to pass. Fine detail cannot be distinguished when viewed through a TRANSLUCENT layer. If detail can be observed through a colored layer, it is often called TRANSPARENT. See also OPAQUE. Example: PP46 Heart.

TRANSPARENT. Clear (colorless) or with color that allows fine detail to be distinguished when viewed through it. See also TRANSLUCENT and OPAQUE. Example: 1980B.

TWIST. A millefiori rod made by encasing colored glass rods within clear glass, then twisting the rod during the pulling or stretching process. See also RIBBON.

TWIST CANE. See TWIST.

UPRIGHT BOUQUET. A bouquet of three-dimensional flowers or fruits set in a vertical layout.

UPSET MUSLIN. See LACE.

WEIGHT. See PAPERWEIGHT.

183

About the Authors

Colin Mahoney, a graduate of California State Polytechnic University at Pomona, is an Electrical Engineer at NASA's Jet Propulsion Laboratory, where he designs spacecraft instrumentation. His instruments have flown on missions such as Mars Pathfinder and the Galileo mission to Jupiter.

Debby Mahoney graduated from Principia College in Elsah, Illinois, in Business Administration and Economics. Following graduation, she managed voice, data, and security communications for a Florida financial institution. She now works at the Jet Propulsion Laboratory as a financial analyst.

On a trip to Florida in conjunction with a space program, Colin bought his first paperweight—a Perthshire. He also met Debby in Florida. The relationships, both with Debby and with Perthshire, grew. Colin and Debby's collection now includes all of Perthshire's Annual Collection paperweights and many Limited Edition and General Range weights.

Recognized as experts on Perthshire paperweights, the Mahoneys were personally invited by Neil Drysdale to spend a week at the Perthshire factory, photographing and doing research.

Gary and Marge McClanahan met at the University of Wisconsin, where they both played in the symphony orchestra. After earning a degree in Naval Science (Chemical Engineering), Gary spent six years in the U.S. Marine Corps as a fighter/attack pilot. He now is a Captain with American Airlines.

Marge's degree in Chemistry led to a career in advanced battery development and program management in the aerospace/defense industry. She is now retired and devotes her full time to the McClanahan's paperweight business.

Gary and Marge began their "serious" collecting with Perthshire weights. They first visited Perthshire in 1982. Soon Gary was a Perthshire dealer, and in 1991 he became a registered Paperweight Collectors Association (PCA) dealer. The McClanahans now have a complete Perthshire collection.

The Mahoneys and the McClanahans first met each other in 1988 at a Southern California PCA meeting. At the time, both couples had acquired most of the Annual Collection weights. As their collections grew, the "thrill of the chase" became the basis of a lasting friendship and a familiarity with Perthshire that eventually led to this book.